BRILLIANT

BRILLIANT:
WHITE
IN
DESIGN
LINDA O'KEEFFE
THE MONACELLI PRESS

To Annie Lineham, Anne Fegent, and Anne McDonnell

Library of Congress Cataloging-in-Publication Data
O'Keeffe, Linda, date.
Brilliant : white in design / Linda O'Keeffe. — 1st ed.
p. cm.
ISBN 978-1-58093-324-7
1. Color in design. 2. White. I. Title. II. Title: White in design.
NK1548.O39 2011
701'.85—dc23   2011016845

Printed in China

www.monacellipress.com

10 9 8 7 6 5 4 3 2 1
First edition

Designed by Claudia Brandenburg, Language Arts

According to a team of Johns Hopkins astronomers who surveyed the electromagnetic radiation emitted by two hundred thousand galaxies, the color of the universe has changed over the last ten billion years. Using a color spectrum chart, they calculated the atmosphere's chromatic evolution from pale turquoise to its current shade, a white that falls between beige and cream. They debated whether to christen the color "univeige" or "skyvory," but after a trip to a local coffee shop, they settled on "cosmic latte."

The notion that the earth's atmosphere is composed of invisible, off-white molecules comes as no surprise to anyone who regards white as a non-color. After all, it stands to reason that if black is the absorption of all colors then white is its insipid, bleached counterpart.

In reality, white contains all colors, a notion widely debated by philosophers and theologians for centuries until Sir Isaac Newton confirmed it as fact in the late 1600s. In a darkened room he observed a narrow beam of white light split into colors as it passed through a prism and reassemble into white as it passed through a second prism. His experiment defined white light as an equally proportioned combination of all the visible colors of the spectrum reflected in the eye.

As if to amplify the whiteness of the atmosphere and the human optic range, white buildings—from the elevated architecture of marble temples, cathedral spires, and mosque minarets to humble whitewashed adobes, barns, and cottages—have been indigenous to most cultures since ancient times. White floors, walls, and roofs are a staple of every climate: they rebuff the heat and diffuse bright light, or they act as an antidote to dark, cold climates.

A white porch or picket fence conjures a nostalgic charm, but white is equally at home in a futuristic spaceship; and when it governs an interior space, its range of moods is enormous. It can be calming or confrontational, sterile or sensual, humble or sophisticated, cerebral or down-to-earth, puritanical or decadent, chameleon-like or egotistical. No other color shares white's versatility. As a result, whether it is used in architecture, design, fashion, or art, white transcends the comings and goings of modish trends. White is immune to fads. It is perpetually modern and permanently "in."

Today's abundance of white paint colors connects back to the mid-nineteenth century when lead pigment, at that time procured by acid corrosion in the presence

Pure forms show the spectrum of white's potential. An immaculate pearl symbolizes anything from wisdom to rapture. A cased glass tumbler is destined to contain milk. A paper-thin ivory spoon is too delicate for practical use, while a bone spoon is obliquely shaped to feed a small child. An unglazed porcelain spoon absorbs strong food colors. A pre-coronation doll's head of Elizabeth II traces its lineage back to Elizabeth I, the Virgin Queen. A carved Chinese figurine once preserved female modesty in a doctor's office.

of carbon dioxide, gave way to zinc oxide. Since paints were then sold by weight and lead is as heavy as it is toxic, the introduction of zinc made paint affordable and therefore available to a wider slice of the population. Around 1916, titanium dioxide, which in its pure state reflects more than 90 percent of direct light, gave white paint its brilliance. Household paint manufacturers continually add to their already extensive catalogs of white paint. New shades vary infinitesimally from their predecessors and carry evocative names like minced onion, cotton whisper, wet cement, November rain, and moonrise.

Like the brilliant cut of a diamond, the title of this book pegs white's many facets and its spectrum not only of colors but also of talents. *Brilliant: White in Design* strives to explain why white has had such vibrant appeal, through the centuries and today. Each chapter looks at white through a different lens, exploring its potentials and, at times, its weaknesses.

"White" and "light" share linguistic roots. As words and concepts, they are often used synonymously by poets, writers, and artists. Designers and architects are particularly drawn to white's ability to showcase their work in its most pure, most elemental form.

As as an antidote to commotion, chaos, and cacophony, white is the color of choice for anyone who craves equilibrium in a work or living space. White is the universal poster child for purity and innocence. It exemplifies cleanliness in the form of a crisp white shirt, a bleached linen tablecloth, a porcelain bathroom tile, a marble kitchen counter.

White demands upkeep; to hoteliers, restaurateurs, and retailers, it is a color of extravagance, drama, and high marketability. A born diplomat, white unites disparate elements of clothing, design, and architecture into one cohesive family. In the hands of certain interior designers, off-whites and beiges lose their mass appeal and become elegant and sophisticated.

Since time immemorial, white, the reigning color of high-mindedness and contemplation, has had associations with places of spiritual practice, and white, as it occurs in nature, is awe-inspiring, mysterious, and mythical. Literally and figuratively, in the words of designer Barbara Barry, "much more than a color, white is a state of mind."

In winter the snow-drifted mountains of the Shiretoko Peninsula, a remote northeastern corner of the Japanese island Hokkaido, are accessible only on foot or by air. Vincent Munier's photograph displays these white and pristine slopes. "Would that life were the shadow cast by a wall or tree, but it is the shadow of a bird in flight," reads the Talmud.

RADIANT:
IT ALL BEGINS AND ENDS WITH WHITE

SHADOW IS A COLOR AS LIGHT IS, BUT LESS BRILLIANT.
PAUL CÉZANNE

Perforated-steel stair treads cast an intricate, dramatic shadow onto the white stucco entrance wall of the Kalfus Studio in Los Angeles, the first freestanding house designed by architect Steven Ehrlich.

White light is primordial. When a newborn baby first opens its eyes, white, shapeless light seeps in; soon the whiteness, in the words of designer Michael Wolfson, "gives life to shadows." As vision continues to develop, it draws a connection between light and dark and sculpts a dimensional world. By all accounts, people who have had near-death experiences recall a pull toward a tunnel of white light. In other words, life begins and ends with white.

The psychological connections to those preverbal white light revelations are anything but fleeting. "Whether we are aware of it or not," says color expert Laura Guido-Clark, "part of us will always perceive light and shade as fundamentally familiar and, to some degree, comforting." According to one theory, babies perceive the shifting of the sun's light as existing solely for their amusement, which makes that "play" of light their first foray into actual play.

Black-and-white imagery often freeze-frames those early sense memories. At the outset of his career, architect David Ling recalls being affected by Alexander Rodchenko and László Moholy-Nagy, whose early-twentieth-century photographs relied on shadow as a main protagonist. "Without the distraction of color," says Ling, "my focus sharpened and cut straight to matters of form, composition, and texture." Product designers similarly acknowledge the ability of white to distill their work down to a dialogue between shape, light, and shadow, which then evolves into a celebration of the chosen material.

The fundamental connection between white, light, and dark is at the core of architect Richard Meier's work. "Whiteness creates a neutral surface on which to build an experience of a space. It heightens one's awareness of the organization and ordering principles of the space," he says. "It allows the powerful play of light and shadow to come to expression in the most expansive way."

White has a particular three-dimensional resonance for other architects, like Steven Holl, who refers to the "music of architecture" that is visible when he walks through an open, predominantly white space, "while arcs of sunlight beam white light and shadow."

White, to interior designer Orlando Diaz-Azcuy, is just as foundational. "It is how I begin a project," he says, "and it's often how I end."

Tony Duquette created this white-plaster, wall-mounted assemblage of twigs and Roman ruins for the Beverly Hills salon of costume designer Adrian in the early 1940s. Duquette recognized the dramatic value of a shadow cast by white but preferred festive decoration and color. "There's nothing calming in these all-white rooms," he once said. "In fact, they make me very nervous."

In *Kitchen*, an ongoing photography series by Laura Hull, white and shadow infuse drama into a normally overlooked detail—the intersection of two cupboards and two drawers—in her Los Angeles loft. Enlarged, the space becomes a structural crossroads.

Jean-Marc Gady's experience as an interior designer, teacher, and creative director for Louis Vuitton informs his witty French Cancan lamp. A steel structure turns eight generic lampshades into a seventy-inch halo of white light that is equal parts Folies Bergère and Ferris wheel.

When asked to convert a five-thousand-square-foot car park into a temporary, covered entrance for the 2010 Design Miami fair, architects Moorhead & Moorhead designed a structure from standard white vinyl panels. A series of folds and hand-cut slits transformed the panels into a latticework canopy that casts deep, complex shadows onto the lot's gleaming white floor.

Arabesque- and Islamic-
patterned window screens
carved from gleaming white
Makrana marble are dotted
throughout the Taj Mahal
and other Mughal buildings.
For a table Paul Mathieu
designed for Odegard,
Rajasthani craftsmen pierced
a cylinder—a hollowed-
out slab of marble—until it
resembled a diaphanous
piece of white lace.

As snow accumulates, it is compressed into heaps of clear ice crystals. Sunlight reflects off the snow and scatters all the colors of the spectrum in every conceivable direction. The eye perceives these millions of mirrored facets as white. Vincent Munier's photograph captures this effect in a remote mountain range. "In a physical paradox," wrote Lysiane Ganousse of the image, "snow weighs heavily on things and lightens them at the same time."

White, light, and shade at once soften and define angles. Furniture and product designer Martha Sturdy's ghostly armchair is a hollow mold of one-inch-thick white resin lit from within. Her chandelier drips with spaghetti-thin strips of the same substance.

True to his modernist roots, Price Harrison's buildings are stark raving white down to the smallest detail. In this Nashville house, the architect cut a series of geometric shapes into white sheetrock at the base of a two-story stairwell to animate an otherwise ordinary wall.

The pristine whiteness of Richard Schultz's iconic outdoor furniture belies its durability. The collection derives its name from the year of its design, 1966, and is currently made by B&B Italia from Teflon-threaded seats, porcelain, and powder-coated steel.

Epoxy floors, a translucent acrylic desk, and a room divider emphasize the radiant qualities of Tracy Kendall's three-dimensional wallpaper in architect Rene Gonzalez's transformation of this Miami office.

In the renovation of a Manhattan townhouse, Tsao & McKown celebrated the house's 150-year-old ovoid staircase by illuminating it from above. The inspiration for the circular light well came from the architects' "childhood amazement at first seeing the nearly invisible, dematerialized dome of a planetarium ceiling bathed in even, white light." A suspended fishing net childproofs the stair.

Oscar Niemeyer's National Museum in Brasília has been called an architectural conceit because its white interior rarely, if ever, exhibits anything. According to writer Peter Godfrey, Niemeyer's trademark use of white reflects his "aim to convey beauty and harmony through the simple geometry of the structure itself, rather than adornment and decoration." Lynn Davis, known for her photographs of natural and constructed wonders, here focuses on the building's sinuous arches and gravity-defying walkway.

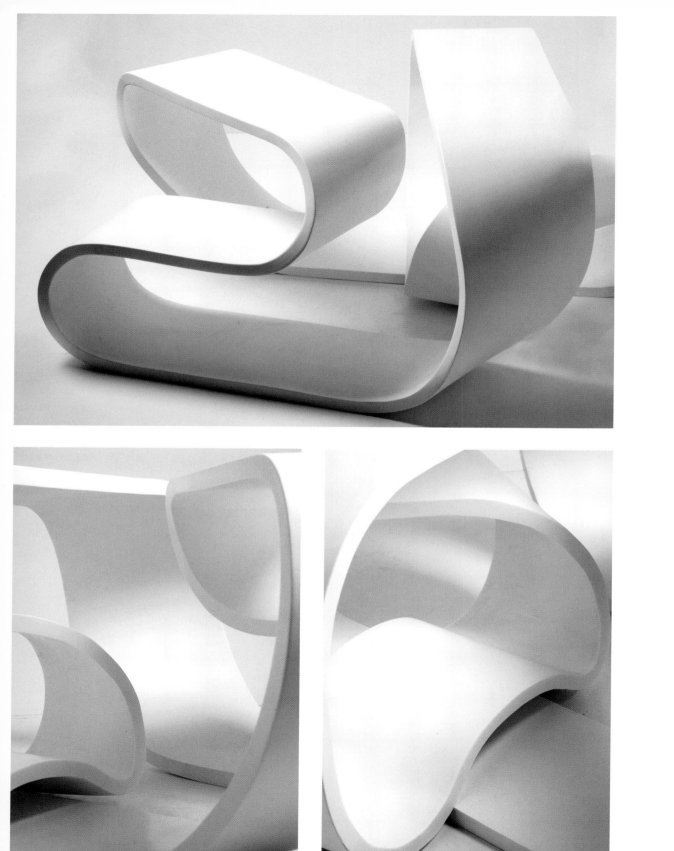

The same medium—Glacier White Corian—in different hands yielded complementary opposites. Created in 2008, Karim Rashid's seven-foot-long Endless Nile, a functional counter with built-in seating, resembles a futuristic picnic table. The ribbon of thermoformed material undulates and redefines itself from every perspective. For a Chicago exhibition, "Exercises in Another Material," the Milan-based industrial design firm Sottsass Associates created Capital, a seven-foot-tall angular column that might moonlight as a minimalist dovecote. Ettore Sottsass, more typically known for designing with vivid colors and patterned laminates, once said, "You don't save your soul just painting everything white."

A guest once speculated that walking into Zaha Hadid's all-white London penthouse might induce an "attack of snow blindness." The same could be said of the Burnham Pavilion, a temporary structure she designed in Chicago in 2009 to house a multimedia installation. Photographer Michelle Litvin represents the Iraqi-born architect's geometric manipulations of space, which created a complex skeleton of bent aluminum overlaid, inside and out, with a light-modulating, white, tensile fabric.

Israeli designer Ron Arad's stackable Tom Vac chair, constructed from injection-molded thermoplastics and produced by Vitra, generates light patterns similar to those of the raked sand of a Japanese Zen garden.

Light and shadow exaggerate the fluidity of Messana O'Rorke's sculptural plaster staircase. The contoured shell conforms to the footprint of a preexisting staircase that punctuated the core of a duplex apartment on Manhattan's Upper West Side; a wall of frosted glass lights the faces of Hans-Peter Krafft's woolly sheep.

The white matte version of Verner Panton's S chair is a contoured vehicle for light and shadow. An engineering degree and a penchant for radical, psychedelic interiors led the Dutch designer to create the unconventional 1960 design that is considered to be the first injection-molded chair.

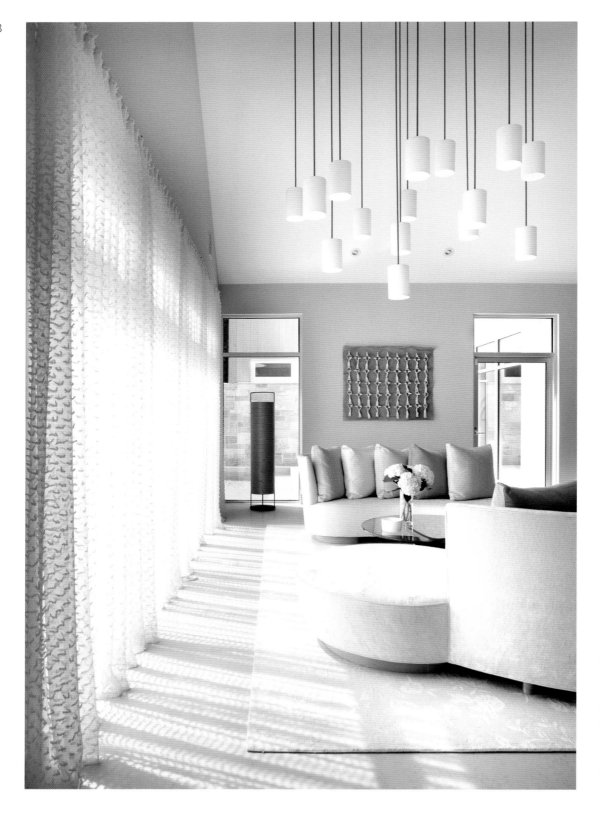

Rooms that boast a wealth of natural light take best to lamps, sconces, or chandeliers that are strong, sculptural objects in their own right. John Wigmore's formation of Japanese paper cylinders, suspended low on steel rods, humanizes the scale of the eighteen-foot ceilings in a Hamptons house designed by architect Bruce Nagel. Interior designer Betty Wasserman used a tranquil range of ivories, creams, and whites throughout the house, but the living room's window wall, dressed in yards of Larsen's cloud-covered sheers, is her most dramatic gesture.

This space, on a narrow floor of a triplex in Chelsea, New York, has an open floor plan by architect Eric Gartner; lighting designer Todd Rugee defined the width of the dining room with a lead crystal chandelier that mirrors the length of the table. Interior designer Charles Allem's all-white furnishings and extensive use of mirrors attract light from the Hudson River.

White and shadow express the historical layering Alison Sky infused into her 1986 renovation of an 1820s Manhattan house. Sky, a founding partner of SITE, attached elements she salvaged from the interior demolition of Laurie Mallet's three-story house onto its new, white stucco walls. Cast characters—a mantel, a door surround, a severed chair, a bottle, a stack of books— emerge from a hallway or retreat into a sheetrock threshold. Thanks to a consistent use of white, the small house feels cohesive and spacious, and Sky's device has stood the test of time. "The objects aren't spooky," says Mallet, "they're still friendly and the white is appeasing."

Each aspect of the bedroom Tori Golub designed in a Showtime show house for the lead character of the comedic drama *United States of Tara* has meaning. The white and black scheme emphasizes the light and dark aspects of Tara's multiple personalities; deep folds in a dupioni silk and velvet bedspread correspond to her shadowy psyche; Ian Gonsher's Table Displaced, a wooden stool encased in an acrylic cube, illustrates her off-kilter imaginings; and a flock of silk butterflies hammered onto the padded headboard is a literal reference to Tara's need to escape.

An installation constructed from scrim, ambient light, and white walls occupied the core of John Pawson's "Plain Space," a 2011 retrospective exhibition at London's Design Museum. Despite its apparent void, design journalist Suzanne Trocmé found the piece to be reassuringly complete. "Pawson understands that we are phototropic, that we walk toward light, then take refuge in shadows—the umbra and the penumbra in between," she says. "For some people, that evokes a spiritual experience, but for me, it evokes an experience that's extremely grounded and logical."

32

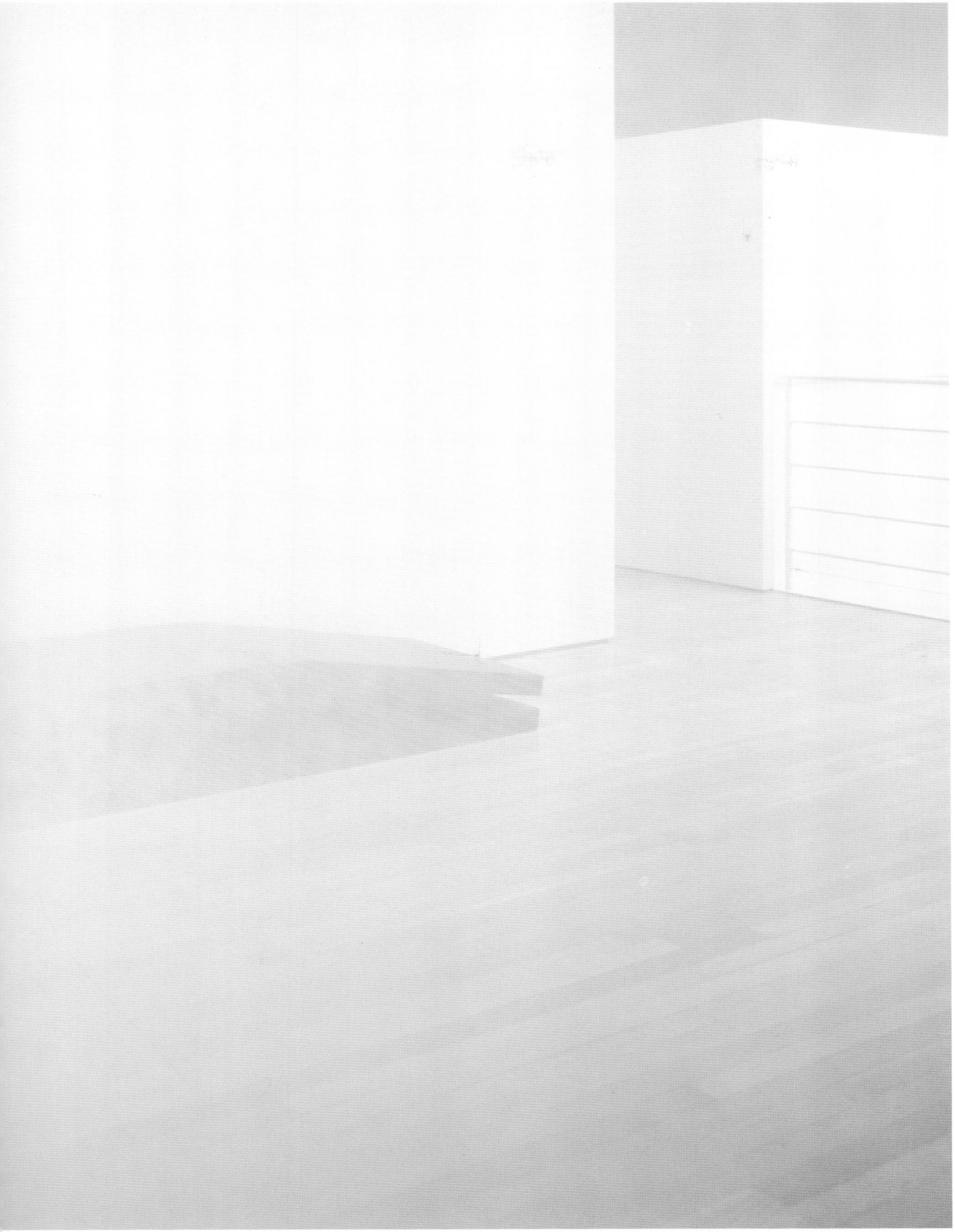

Silver Rain, a La Prairie spa designed by D'Aquino Monaco in the Cayman Islands, is a light and sound experience that is both calming and invigorating. As a nod to La Prairie's leitmotif, a glacier, allusions to water appear throughout the silvery white interiors. Metaphorically, the liquid gushes beneath tiled floors; swirls across walls in the guise of crushed silk; and trenches across carved Thalweg panels that exploit light and render deep, rhythmic shadows.

At Hotel Azúcar, a compound of whitewashed bungalows overlooking the Gulf of Mexico, white conveys a sense of back-to-basics simplicity. Designer Carlos Couturier installed rustic, outdoor showers that catch the shadows of latticed awnings and thatched roofs and named each of the white-on-white rooms after a Veracruz sugar mill.

A system of manually operable white mesh screens simultaneously encases and animates this research building outside of Berlin. Glass Kramer Löbbert Architects designed the metal sheath to filter sunlight, conceal balconies, and slipcover the glass and honeycomb-brick understructure. Entirely closed, the screens enable the building to conform to a regimented rectangle; randomly opened, they transform it into a giant three-dimensional rendition of a snowy Advent calendar.

OVERLEAF
Light streaming through a skylight fifty-five feet above ground paints motion onto a central staircase in this late-nineteenth-century Manhattan townhouse. Architect Donald Billinkoff eliminated the original stairway and its traditional logic of switchbacks and floor-to-floor runs in favor of a three-foot-wide rhythmic sculpture that wends its way through five stories. Constructed off site from steel, medium-density fiberboard, and white Corian, the undersides of the risers and treads are illuminated at night.

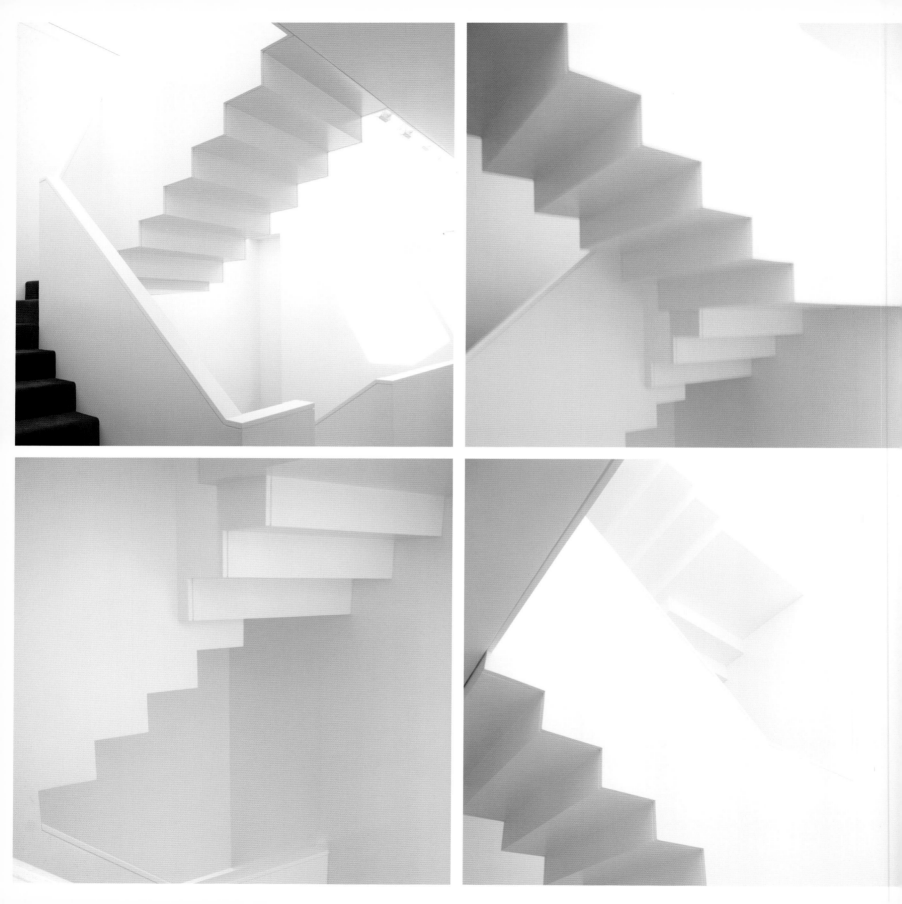

PURE:
PRISTINE AND (UN)CORRUPTED

Filmmaker and artist John Waters's 2001 *Sneaky J.F.K.* questions, in Waters's usual tongue-in-cheek manner, whether President John F. Kennedy was ever jealous enough of his wife's status as a style icon to dress up in her clothes. "I'm radical and right-wing about some things," says Waters, "and wearing white after Labor Day is definitely a fashion faux pas. So is wearing velvet before Thanksgiving and patent shoes before Easter."

I USED TO BE SNOW WHITE, BUT I DRIFTED.

MAE WEST

The designers and architects in Orlando Diaz-Azcuy's luxuriously white San Francisco office wear white lab coats to preserve the purity of the fabric and paint samples they handle all day. "White gives you the opportunity to see all colors by comparison," says Diaz-Azcuy.

In Western cultures, white is worn to manifest inner purity and innocence—an immaculate christening gown, a chaste choirboy's robe, a novice's judo belt. In 1840, Queen Victoria initiated a now-commonplace tradition when she chose a white wedding gown. Subsequently, the custom of European queens donning white when they entered into deep mourning—which dated back to medieval times—died out. In China, Japan, and parts of Africa, funeral-goers still dress in white to pay respect to the virtuousness of the departing soul.

At various times throughout history, white clothing replaced bathing when hygiene was not considered important and when bathtubs were portable and unassigned to one particular room. Nowadays, white is popularly accepted as the color best suited to the daily rituals of cleansing, and it ranks as the color of choice in most bathrooms.

Le Corbusier, one of the most influential architects of the twentieth century, saw white as supremely hygienic. He often wore a white doctor's coat when he expressed his belief that white walls had the power to eradicate the past and promote an inner "chastity," "virginity," and "decency." Anyone who painted a room entirely white, he believed, strived for perfection and a state of high morality.

The architect's iconic Villa Savoye, built in 1925 and subsequently named a National Monument of France, contained "no dirty, dark corners." As a symbolic statement, he mounted a white, freestanding sink in the entrance hallway. Visitors encounter it as they enter the house the way parishioners encounter a holy water font when they cross the threshold of a Catholic church.

However, not all designers advocate the use of white. An accumulation of dust might romanticize a colored surface; on white, it reads as grubby, a fact that's not lost on designer Michael Wolfson. "Remember," he warns clients who fantasize about white's incorruptibility, "today's white is tomorrow's gray." Colorist Bruno Taut, who practiced architecture long before self-cleaning building materials became available, liked to pontificate similarly. "A white house," he would say, "after a certain time, looks as if it is wearing a dirty white shirt."

Of course, a dirty white shirt is not beyond repair. Laundry is a preoccupation in designer Benjamin Noriega-Ortiz's whiter-than-white duplex apartment in Manhattan, but he conceals the washer and dryer he keeps in his foyer. "Living in a white apartment and keeping it clean has its limitations and sacrifices," he says. "We remove our shoes and street clothes because being home is a sublime experience. In that way, we treat our space as if it is a temple."

Eileen Gray's tailored
furniture and Yves Saint
Laurent's detailed couture
clothing inspired the
bathroom fixtures Bill Sofield
designed for Kallista.
The stucco basin, vanity
in Blanche Lacquer,
and honed marble counter
are crafted to be both
pure and precious.

The sense of airiness in this corner of a Manhattan master bedroom, designed by Tori Golub, stems from an exploration of materials and shapes. The concrete base of Ingo Maurer's Wo-tum-bu lamp contrasts with the delicacy of its twisted paper shade; Barlas Baylar's richly polished, cast-bronze side table owes its texture and indentations to a chunk of wood; Hans J. Wegner's solid Ox chair and ottoman reads as lightweight and leggy when upholstered in white wool bouclé.

Despite their starched white look, the furnishings Toby Zack chose for this twenty-eight-foot-high circular living room in Palm Beach are entirely user-friendly. Lacquered cabinetry, leather and shag rugs, and outdoor-grade upholstery are all extremely low maintenance, and the extra-deep sofas encourage guests to take their shoes off and recline.

Kelly Hoppen instills a sense of ritual into her bathroom designs: flattering, creamy white is invariably highlighted by dark surfaces. In a converted London loft that once housed a school gymnasium, Hoppen allotted almost as much space to the spalike bathroom as she did to the adjoining master bedroom. "Cream is the most tranquil of colors," she says.

The grand sense of procession in this Parisian bathroom, designed by Pierre Yovanovitch, belies its small size. Despite the boudoir elegance of Tommi Parzinger's chandelier and Harvey Probber's marble table, the seamlessly integrated marble sink and tub project the formality of a public fountain.

Benjamin Noriega-Ortiz designed this glamorous white Hamptons dining room with eminent practicality in mind. The faux-leather upholstery cleans with a wipe, and cotton slipcovers are easily bleached. Seven chain-mail chandeliers span the ceiling, allowing tables and seating to be reconfigured at whim under even light.

Along with a cleansing visual pause, Noriega-Ortiz instilled an illusion of space into a small hallway in this Miami house. Rendered in the same bone white as the background wall, a Victorian chair slips into the guise of sculpture; the focal play of a tiny mirror in a wide circular frame draws the eye and underscores the poetry of the scalloped plaster archway.

The crisp white lines of a Ridgefield, Connecticut, kitchen have chic connotations for its designer, Lynne Scalo. "This room is like the quintessential 'little white dress' in that everything is exactly scaled and tailored," she says, likening the white Venetian plaster walls to freshly painted nails. Southeastern light amplifies the white swirls in the poured-resin table and bounces off the rock-crystal chandelier.

Much of the available
western light is blocked from
this Brian Murphy–designed
bathroom by an adjacent
covered patio. The architect
chose a white palette and
a slew of mirrors to harvest
any available light.

Thanks to a large rectangular mirror, the vibrant white interior of this Monterey, California, bathroom borrows a green tinge from the canyon garden outside. Catherine Fellowes designed the room with architect Cynthia Carlson using white Thassos marble, porcelain, and a customized Farrow & Ball Strong White paint.

A vast family of whites underscores the inherent luxury of this master bedroom suite, which commands a floor in a Georgian terrace house in London. René Dekker's palette of creams, ivories, and parchments manifests in every conceivable texture and material. Wall coverings range from moiré paper to pearlized tile; faux-leather upholstery mimics crocodile or kid; crystals button the headboard.

In Seattle, architect Stuart Silk floated an oversized Waterworks tub on a sea of Carrara marble tiles to visually increase the size of a small bathroom.

In Charles Allem's Miami apartment, the sensual curves of Arne Jacobsen's Egg chair are a perfect foil for the oversized, angular headboard.

Unlined white curtains and large paper lanterns offset the formality of the coved ceiling in the dining room of Catherine Fellowes's Silver Lake, Los Angeles, house.

In designer Laurie Owen's unpretentious Johannesburg bathroom, a sheepskin bathmat complements the rusticity of a group of tree stumps and wicker baskets. Her versatile tub/shower accommodates pets as well as people.

In the kitchen of Tricia Foley's weekend house on Long Island, New York, bare windows admit southern light and views of a white shed, studio, and chicken coop. Salvaged kitchen cabinets store linens and a mix of eighteenth-century and Ikea china. "White gives me a blank canvas that I change according to the season," says Foley, who repaints the table every summer. "Flowers in the summer, twigs in the fall, and sheepskin rugs over the chairs in the winter."

Natural light, tracked in via cut-out rectangles in the ceiling of this house in Strasbourg, France, blankets the white walls and limestone floors, highlighting different areas throughout the day. The overall space never fragments because white is so absolute.

According to design maven Barbara Marshall, "White is a denial of the messiness of our humanity." In the age of wireless technology, there's less debate in the interior design community about keeping electronic equipment out of plain sight. A white television set blends into the all-white decor of a Hamptons, New York, house and becomes another element in the landscape.

In the Manhattan apartment Benjamin Noriega-Ortiz shares with his partner, Steven Wine, a night table lamp covered in turkey feathers flaunts its coiled cord.

Designer Kara Mann's bedroom on Chicago's Lake Shore Drive faces south to a view of the city. The designer loves murky, dark colors but sleeps in a radiant white canopy bed hung with sheers that bear names like Ballerina and Edelweiss. Southern light reflecting off neighboring buildings gives the room a pink undertone. Consequently, says the designer, "I always wake up feeling like the sun is shining in my face."

In the master bathroom of a Marfa, Texas, house once owned by designer Barbara Hill, a rectangular soaking tub takes pride of place. White Diamond plaster gives a chalky, suedelike texture to the adobe walls and adds dimension to the small space.

A rectangular Parsons table centered on a translucent, shade-covered window governs the dining room of a Florida house designed by Toby Zack. The light and shapes gain greater prominence in the reflections on the marble floor.

The stark whiteness and angularity of this Houston house, designed by Price Harrison, was informed by the owner's art collection, which includes works by Ellsworth Kelly, Josef Albers, and Brice Marden. In the east-facing dining room, floor-to-ceiling draperies, white leather upholstery, and waterborne-finished maple floors create a white envelope.

In a Nashville house, the sheetrock and marble partition Harrison devised to separate the living and dining rooms evolved into a piece of sculpture that houses a fireplace and storage that serve both spaces.

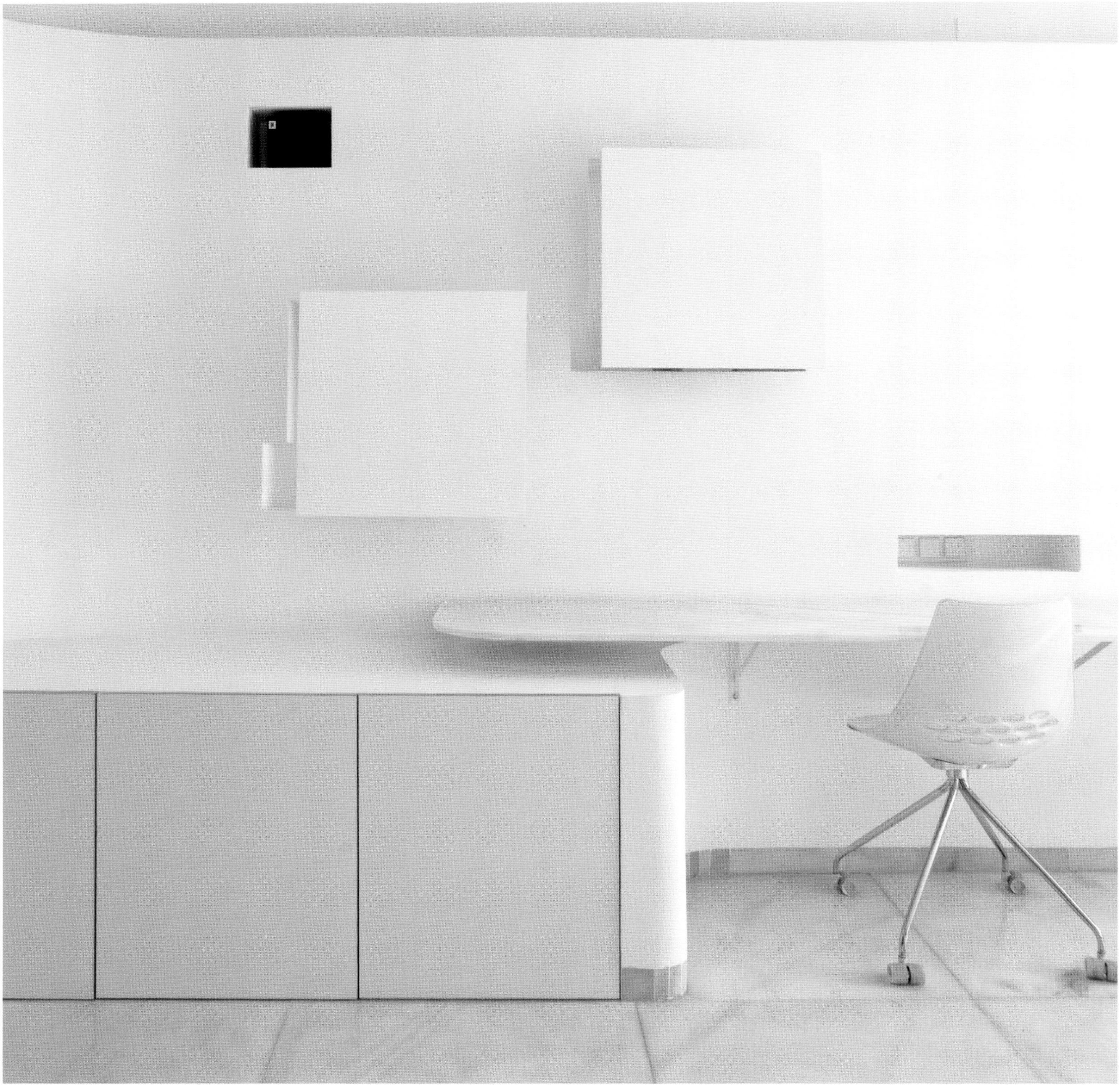

If necessary, the movable partitions that form the perimeter wall of this open loft in the historic center of Valencia, Spain, easily configure the space into conventional rooms. Sergio Bruns and Pruden Arnau sculpted edges, eliminated hardware, and mirrored doors to allow the space's white Macael marble floors to attract any light that emanates from the narrow streets of Barrio del Carmen. As architect Alberto Campo Baeza once said, "Light is more."

OVERLEAF
In 2008 in the gritty industrial French port of Le Havre, architect Jean Nouvel designed Les Bains des Docks, a public aquatic center that is part lap pool, part Roman bath, part lagoon. Despite its rigorous composition of blocky, bleached terrazzo elements and expansive glass walls, visitors primarily hear the sound of water as it pours, streams, and trickles among a series of white whirlpools, falls, and fountains.

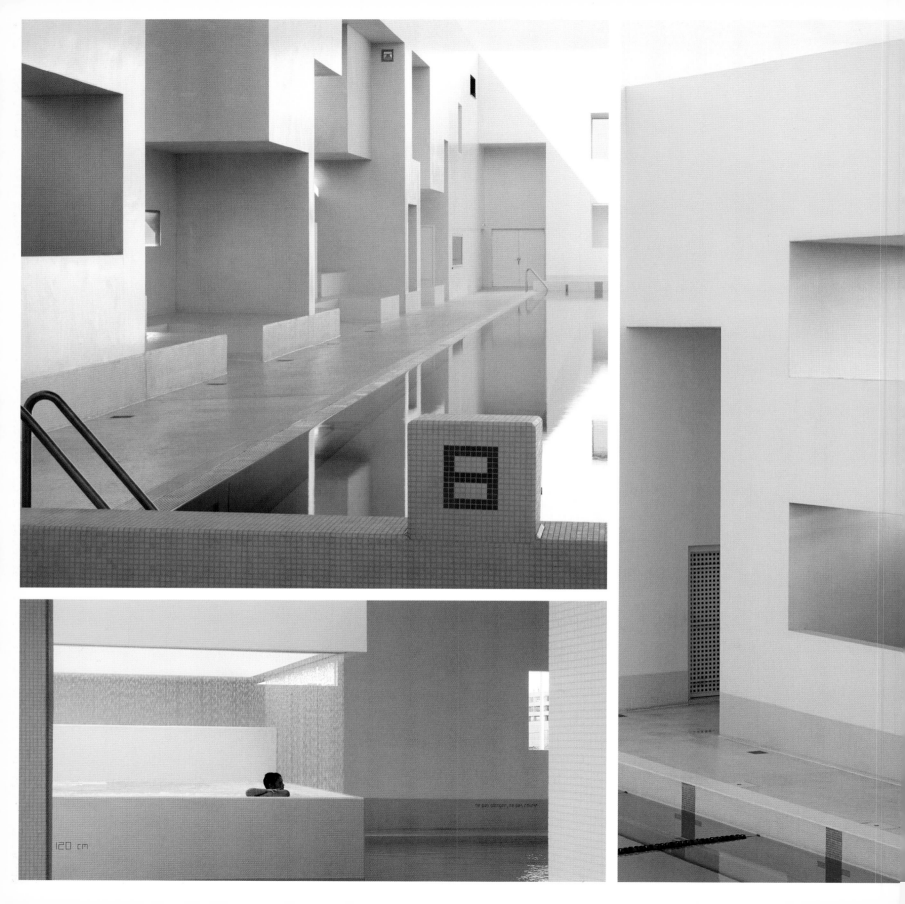

120 cm

SEDUCTIVE:
THE COVETOUS COLOR

By day the etched-glass facade of Cannelle, the London cake shop John Pawson designed in 1988, filtered light into the bakery. By night, a local newspaper noted, it glowed like a "spectral light box." The architect inserted a clear glass cube in the center of the facade to provide a royal showcase for a single gâteau. At first the minimalist statement struck some onlookers as confrontational and anti-retail, but it was soon perceived as a cleverly distilled marketing tool.

> **WHITE IS A SNOB THAT LIKES ITS OWN COMPANY BEST.**
> JANICE LINDSAY

White bathrobes, fluffy white towels, and crisp white bed linens are standard attributes of any five-star hotel. When white extends onto walls, floors, curtains, and upholstery, a room reeks of decadence no matter its size. It's a luxurious pad and its occupants join the ranks of the privileged.

The minimalist wave of the mid-1990s peaked when entrepreneur Ian Schrager, along with designer Philippe Starck, unleashed a string of theatrical boutique hotels in the United States and abroad. Spacious, cinematic lobbies—places for visitors to see and be seen—contrast sharply with minuscule, all-white guest accommodations, which

David Hoey, Bergdorf Goodman's director of visual presentation, is inspired by everything from Lewis Carroll to flying machines. His all-white windows are a seasonal favorite and often resemble dioramas from a museum of natural history. On the other hand, they might feature one oversized object or be constructed from mundane articles, like rolls of white paper.

often rival the size of a ship's cabin. One overnight occupant at the Delano in Miami compared his room to an "insane asylum," while another felt he was sleeping in a "cloud."

Around the same time, the Hempel, an off-white London hotel designed by Anouska Hempel using extreme principles of feng shui, was also garnering a great deal of press. When it first opened, its only capitulation to color, aside from its well-manicured Zen garden, was the evening turndown service, which featured a fleshy, green fig. "The desire for white is a desire for control of desire," says writer Mark Quigley, a theory that contradicts the hotel's popularity as a romantic getaway.

Clothing designer Zoran, who has happily occupied white spaces in which a handful of humidifiers take the place of traditional furnishings, sees white as the most self-indulgent of colors: "I live it day in, day out, and so I see how being surrounded by white for long periods of time boosts the ego." He continues, "People and food look best when they're silhouetted against white."

Architect Dirk Denison agrees: Terzo Piano, the restaurant he designed inside the Modern Wing at the Art Institute of Chicago, is entirely white. The color deliberately extends the sedate gallery atmosphere as museum-goers transition into dinner guests. "Instead of observing art against white, they get to people-watch against white, all without the diversion of pattern or color," he says. "And when they are served, the experience changes, and thanks to the white china, the food becomes the star."

Design is the star at Moss, an impeccably curated white store in Manhattan that first opened in 1996. Owner Murray Moss slips into theatrical terminology when he describes his approach to retail. His cutting-edge, innovative merchandise is "on stage," displayed inside vitrines and on white Corian platforms with railings that deter his customers—the "audience"—from close engagement. "White has nothing to do with a desire to be tasteful," says Moss. "The store's white envelope is intended to be a void, a projection screen for people's narratives. White also bounces light and drops shadows, which reveal dimension and form and enforce the museum atmosphere of the display."

The voyeuristic "look but don't touch" vibe has paid off handsomely, and Moss is now world-renowned even though some people find the store's sterile vibe off-putting. "In this environment, apprehension and hesitation are a good thing," he says. "If someone looks at a fruit bowl and turns white with fear, that means the bowl's pretty damn good!"

Designer Silvia Lischetti founded Cyrus Company in the 1970s in Brianza, Italy, and now has showrooms in Paris, New York, and elsewhere. She has outfitted hotels in Florence and Nice with her signature white-lacquer-veneered furniture, including the Cassetti cabinet, Elena and Ovalina chairs, and Anfora table. Her hyper-white stores are a hybrid of classic, cute, kitsch, and comfy.

The Delano Hotel first opened in Miami Beach in 1995 as a complex of poolside bungalows and beach-front rooms. Designed by Philippe Starck, the public spaces are still edgy, theatrical, and surreal, while the rooms and spa are pristinely white. "Anyone can build a building that protects people from the heat, sun and cold," Starck has said. "What I am determined to do is to make a stage where people can be sexier and more brilliant, a place where they can awake smarter."

Fashion renegade Rei Kawakubo collaborated with architect Takao Kawasaki on the design of her Manhattan store, where she displays her black Comme des Garçons clothing line against klieglike white. In a space that is equally intriguing and disorienting, a white-enameled steel counter can artfully display a single line of folded T-shirts while black shoes randomly pepper the white floor.

Although the Zurich-based architecture firm Smolenicky & Partner referenced forests and glades of trees in their 2010 pavilion at the Tamina thermal baths, the monumental fluted columns and extreme whiteness conjure instead a vision of cathedrals. Located in Bad Ragaz, a Swiss region dotted with natural springs, the resort encompasses a pool and a sunbathing lawn.

Designed by India Mahdavi with architect Javier Sánchez, the Condesa DF boutique hotel takes its name from the section of Mexico City often compared to Paris's Latin Quarter. White accordion shutters shield each room from the sun shining into the hotel's triangular inner courtyard. "For me," says Mahdavi, "white is the symbol of absolute neutrality and the projection of all possibilities."

When the landscaping matures, the white concrete walls of a center for biodiversity on the outskirts of Loja, Granada, will merge with the agricultural surroundings. Architects Tomás García Píriz and José Luis Muñoz built an underground corridor of offices that traces the footprint of an abandoned farmstead and sits in the shade of a mature tree. One of the building's entrances, an alluring flight of steep white steps, is described by locals as "a stairway to heaven."

New York Times writer Cintra Wilson speculated that the design of Mauboussin, a jewelry store on New York's Madison Avenue, could be attributed to "Jean Cocteau's Freudian analyst on a laudanum bender." In fact, David Rockwell—who designs everything from playgrounds to Broadway musical sets—was responsible for turning the building's third-floor bridal suite into, in his words, an "ultimate dream wedding, with a twist!" His upholstered walls, crinoline tulle ceiling, tufted sofas, and ostrich-feather screens turn choosing diamond engagement rings into celestial events.

Ice hotels and chill rooms are standard winter fare in Sweden and Finland, but to the uninitiated they still rank as novelties. One method of building the freestanding structures involves framing rooms in steel and spraying on snow. Alternatively, the spaces are constructed from harvested blocks of ice, while creature comforts like electricity are wired in.

Located in Ann Siang Hill, a posh section of Singapore, the Club Hotel has tongue-in-cheek colonial references sprinkled throughout its decor. Designed by Colin Seah's firm Ministry Of Design, the walls of the hotel's generously sized suites and hallways are covered in armor-white paint. The oversized statue of Sir Thomas Stamford Raffles, the city's founder, has lost its head to the underskirts of a fabric ceiling.

81

Anouska Hempel is known for designing seductive white bedrooms in houses and hotels throughout the world. For a guest suite in a Wiltshire country estate, she fashioned a four-poster bed out of Indian sandstone and draped its canopy with eighteenth-century French linen.

In a duplex suite in Hempel's eponymous boutique hotel in London, the designer suspended a heavy oak sleeping platform from stainless-steel ceiling rods and encased it in hefty linen sheets. It sways very slightly when mounted and is regarded as the ultimate non-gambling equivalent of a high roller's bed.

Given Maine's snowy winters, the glistening white floor architect Carol Wilson installed in Sarajo, a gallery in a mid-nineteenth-century building in Portland, seems eminently impractical. In reality, the floor's glossy surface, constructed from Lonseal, a highly resilient vinyl, is easy to clean and also acts as a vibrant showcase for the gallery's collection of rare nineteenth-century Asian textiles, Ottoman brocades, Chinese court robes, and Russian chintzes.

Andrée Putman designed a snowy white Manhattan store to flatter Anne Fontaine's signature white blouses and shirts. The backlit white collar gallery epitomizes the designer's knack for marrying wit, beauty, and access with her belief that people provide the color in monochrome spaces.

When Murray Moss first opened his Soho design store in the mid-1990s, he likened his stark white interiors to an art museum. In its current, renovated incarnation, he refers instead to a museum of natural history, albeit one that sells products ranging from cups to bathtubs. Moss considers white to be the ultimate merchandising vehicle. "It arouses the senses, and it creates both a vacuum and a barrier," he says, "very much like a white matte frame on a photograph manipulates the eye to focus on what's inside."

Terzo Piano, the third-floor restaurant in the Modern Wing of the Art Institute of Chicago, looks out onto Lake Michigan. Designed by Dirk Denison in a controlled palette of white, beige, and gray, the grid of white resin tables and the marble bar catch incessant light from three directions throughout the day.

From the outset, Marcel Wanders envisioned the predominantly white rooms and lobby of Miami's Mondrian South Beach Hotel as "the castle of Sleeping Beauty," but *Alice in Wonderland* is arguably the more apt source. The Dutch designer, a born showman who customarily accessorizes his tailored suits with pearl chokers, juggles scale and perception in the lobby; guest rooms have chandeliers that double as showers and Delft-tiled kitchenettes that depict alligators.

Boutique hotelier Ian Schrager commissioned Swiss architects Herzog & de Meuron to design an enclave of apartments and townhouses in Manhattan's Noho district that incorporates all the amenities of a five-star hotel. Schrager himself designed the showroom spaces predominantly in white. Of an interior view, architect Richard Meier said, "What can be bad about this room? I mean, it's all white!"

For a luxury villa in Mallorca, Marcel Wanders concocted a futuristic en suite master bedroom that's as hedonistic as it is sculptural. A light column sheathed in white fiberglass spotlights a tub that is in plain sight of Wanders's king-sized Dream bed; a highly polished Carrara marble floor acts as a room-wide mirror.

Hoto Fudo, a domed noodle restaurant designed by Takeshi Hosaka, stands on a hillside with a view of Mount Fuji in Japan's Yamanashi region. The architect carved out windows and curved acrylic screens to temper the weather; otherwise, the bloblike structure qualifies as a modernist igloo.

Unfurled rolls of stripes, brocades, and jewel-toned velvets usually cover the white cutting table in Rue Herold, a Parisian fabric store. Owner and former stylist Charlotte de la Grandière designed the meticulously white showroom knowing the color would best flatter her selection of upholstery and fashion textiles.

OVERLEAF
Egg whites, coconut, or almond flour might have inspired the sugary white interior of Theurel & Thomas, a San Pedro patisserie—the first in Mexico to specialize in French macarons. Mexican design firm Anagrama conceptualized the space down to the porcelain displays and the assistants' white chef jackets.

LUCID:
AN ERASER FOR THE CLUTTERED MIND

THERE IS ONLY ONE COLOUR, WHITE; ALWAYS POWERFUL SINCE IT IS POSITIVE.
LE CORBUSIER

When Charles Rennie Mackintosh renovated his Victorian terrace house in Glasgow in 1906, he decorated its drawing room entirely in white. His love of nature shows up in the furniture's restrained decoration; Japanese minimalism influenced its lines. The stark room glaringly but silently commented on the cluttered, heavy interiors of his contemporaries.

Like miniskirts and white Courrèges boots, Max Clendinning's austere Islington flat epitomizes the peak of 1960s British modernism. Instead of using a conventional arrangement of furniture, the architect defined his living room with a giant, caterpillar-shaped beanbag sofa and a solitary papier-mâché lamp with the proportions of a lamppost.

Connoisseurs of white—those who live or work in monochrome spaces—find the color's airiness and serenity to be soothing, clarifying, and physiologically undemanding. White offers silent relief when the chaos of everyday life is overwhelming.

Designer Barbara Barry, for instance, feels her neutral house and spare, predominantly white studio support and engender a focused clearheadedness. "White spaces," she says, "encourage us to 'breathe out' when we encounter them."

Similarly, designer Judy Niedermaier saw the white homes she occupied throughout her career as fueling stations that supplied the energy and creativity she needed to design furniture and run her business. "When it comes to describing tranquil interiors, the words 'sanctuary' and 'retreat' are nauseatingly overused," she once said, "but for me they are clichés that absolutely hold true."

Art dealer Olivier Renaud-Clément created his blanched loft as a visual palette cleanser. High ceilings and uncluttered white surfaces offer a relaxing balance to the intensity and focus of his work. "I look at pictures all day long," he says, "and coming home to white offers me the freedom to project, think, and move."

Architect John Pawson once rented an apartment in Japan stuffed with traditional European furniture—which caused a consuming need to create "physical rationality out of the bedlam." He says, "I just needed some neutrality. I wanted to control the environment I was in because I couldn't control what was going on elsewhere." Ever true to his minimalist credo, he painted every square inch of the apartment white, down to its fabric walls.

Oblivious to trends and fashions, white rooms remain eternally modern, a fact that clothing designer Zoran relishes. "I never tire of white," he says. "Over the years, I must have saved millions of dollars because I don't renovate or refurnish, I just retouch!"

According to Doug Levine, who designs interiors as well as furniture, the focus of living in a white apartment is not the color but rather the narrative that emerges from everything, and everyone, that enters the space. "It's about fruit from the market," he says. "It's about the one perfect flower, the silhouette of a woman in black walking down the narrow hall and the glimpse of the red undersole of her shoe. It's about music you play or the echo of a conversation in the next room becoming the foreground to the white background."

"When is the rest of the furniture coming?" or "You actually live like this?" are frequent reactions when people first enter a sparse, white room. "Then, after they've spent some time and fallen in love with the simplicity," explains Levine, "they go home and start purging."

First-time visitors to Olivier Renaud-Clément's loft in Long Island City, New York, routinely tell him they could never live in such extreme whiteness. "I find it to be a peaceful place," he says. "It's a perfect backdrop for everything I do." White also accentuates his patinated collection of vintage Italian furniture designed by the likes of Gae Aulenti, Cini Boeri, and Achille Castiglioni. Architect Steve Blatz created the wide-open 1,500-square-foot space with its single closet door. Renaud-Clément has no desire to warm up the apartment with conventional accessories like floor coverings, pillows, and throws and only has flowers if someone else brings them. "When I think of it," he says, "color scares me!"

Architect Jim Gauer and his partner, Joel Goldsmith, live in a formally modern, twenty-fourth-floor aerie above Victoria's Inner Harbor on Vancouver Island. The west and south exposures take in the Olympic Mountains and catch a quality of light a visitor once likened to an instant cure for seasonal affective disorder. "To my eye," says Gauer, "there's nothing more optimistic than a white room framed against a bright blue sky. The illusion of living in a cloud strikes us as very pleasant."

Beata Galdi's white beach house abuts sand dunes in Amagansett on Long Island, New York, a few steps from the ocean. Skylit channels in the eleven-foot-high ceiling pitch patterns onto the walls of the living room and the adjacent kitchen. Galdi intended the white upholstery, light bamboo floors, white marble counters, and white-lacquered cabinets to exaggerate the space's dimensions and harmonize its flow. "As soon as I arrive here," says the designer, "an automatic mantra sets in: Balance. Rest. Go within."

In the words of design writer Fred Albert, the white interiors of Ron and Anna Rosella's house on Queen Anne Hill in Seattle are "more ermine than ice." After architect Stuart Silk brought cohesion back to the 1901 house by eliminating a warren of disjointed rooms, Anna Rosella painted the living room walls white and brought in art, antiques, and white upholstery. "Seattle gets gloomy in the winter," she says, "and I wanted everything to look crisp when it was gray."

Once described as having
"a virtuosic talent for color,"
designer Kelly Wearstler
customarily paints her hotel
interiors bright yellow and
parrot green. In her own
weekend house in Malibu,
however, she demonstrates
a strong appreciation
for white: western light
bathes an all-white still life
composed of a vintage chair
and two sculptures.

"You can always dip it in
white and it will turn out all
right!" says architect Brian
Murphy, whose work often
showcases his witty and
elevated appropriations of
generic materials. Murphy
once spray-painted a tiny
Santa Monica cottage,
from doorknobs to rafters,
entirely white. "The place
instantly doubled in size,
and it felt plain good to be
inside," he says. "To me,
white is all color."

Toronto designers Powell & Bonnell often rely on textures to achieve a lightweight effect in their white and off-white projects. Here, a nubby, bouclé-upholstered sofa sits near a striated limestone coffee table and simply paneled walls.

In both her furniture designs and her homes, designer Judy Niedermaier repeatedly used white as a touchstone, a fact illustrated in her neutral Chicago condominium, which was located on the forty-ninth floor of one of that city's tallest skyscrapers. Against a simple drywall fire surround, her silky cotton-covered Bardot chairs sat on an undyed wool rug. Ralph Lauren's comment "No matter the trend, no matter what the color of the moment is, I always come back to white" sums up Niedermaier's philosophy.

An expanse of white in an entry sets up expectations of space and light. In this 1963 Hollywood Hills house once owned by designer Darryl Wilson, guests walked through floor-to-ceiling white draperies before glass doors opened into a gleaming circular foyer.

Glossy white enamel on the hallway floor and Benjamin Moore Super White paint on the walls of the loft Steve Blatz designed for Olivier Renaud-Clément fuse into one continuous surface.

Reflective materials and snippets of color give dimension to a white space. In this Dallas sitting room, Blanca Wall of Sojo Design intensified the effects of southern and western light with Lucite, blown glass, and silver accessories.

In Sandra Gering's Greenwich Village, New York, living room, silver blinds, a silver-tinted floor, and a Karim Rashid mirror interact with southern light.

Architect Charles Allem categorizes his Miami apartment as "white and gray, pure and simple"—the direct opposite of the lavish, dramatic, and vivid interiors he frequently designs. Allem, born in South Africa, maintained the color scheme throughout the space's 1,800 square feet to encourage all the rooms to merge into one perfect viewing platform for the jetliners and sunsets over South Beach.

At certain times of the day, eastern light illuminates the white resin table in designer Tori Golub's eighth-floor Manhattan loft. In the evening, internal lights alter the mood. The Serge Mouille ceiling fixture and the backlit wall of white ripple-fold linen sheers create an atmosphere that rivals candlelight.

Vicente Wolf maximized the natural light that floods his large Manhattan loft from three directions by painting walls, floors, and ceiling white and installing white upholstery and a bevy of white objects. "The more shades of white," he says, "the whiter it looks!" Here, a classic eighteenth-century Neapolitan chair guards a plinth full of the Indian-inspired marble vases Wolf designed.

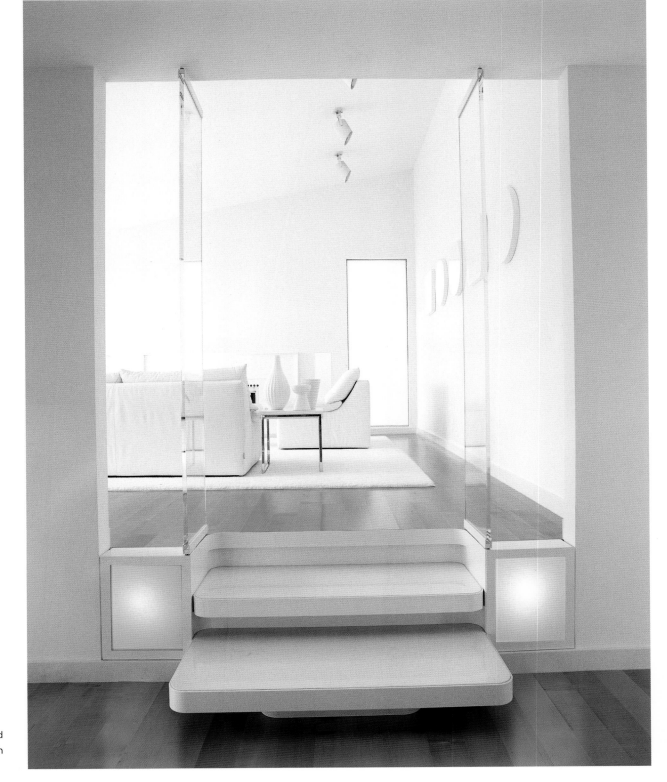

The owners of this Mill Valley, California, house spent most of their working lives in antiseptic white hospitals yet chose white at home for its uplifting, restorative powers. With meticulous attention to detail, designer Daren Joy painted the dining room walls and cabinets glossy white and attached discreet steel door pulls. He recast an awkward transition between the kitchen and dining room as a formal threshold with two floating white marble steps, recessed lighting, and seven-foot-high rotating Plexiglas doors.

In an effort to introduce more light to a living area in their weekend house in Miami, Toronto-based architects George Yabu and Glenn Pushelberg removed various freestanding walls. White surfaces, terrazzo floors, and upholstery, as well as Lucite furniture and stainless-steel art, now lure light from the patio and pool.

In Abigail Turin's San Francisco house, the glass dining room doors open onto a tree-shaded terrace; a vertical window beams southern light onto a crystal chandelier. The designer thinks of the room as a decompression chamber between her charcoal-black living room and her sunflower-yellow kitchen. "White," she says, "is still and always my favorite color."

The flow through this New York apartment along the Hudson River, designed by Carl D'Aquino and Francine Monaco, is ever-changing thanks to a series of polished, matte, and carved sliding panels. A sculptural cabinet houses a motorized television and displays an Eva Hild sculpture. A wall of curtains dressed in Åsa Pärson's Missing Thread textile manipulates the western light that floods in from the river.

Jill Vantosh's method of sequencing wall colors throughout an Atlanta house may seem counterintuitive. In the shaded dining room, she opted for a dark charcoal that often reads as black; in the grand living room, with fourteen-foot ceilings and three exposures, the designer chose bone-white walls, furnishings, and textiles. She explains, "White very simply brought out the beauty of this room."

Located on a street of traditional Art Nouveau buildings in Strasbourg, France, this white cubic house with its double-height windows and vast white living room is calm perfection to its minimalist owners. They chose to orient the room's furniture toward an outside pool and garden rather than a television set.

OVERLEAF

Every room in Michaela Scherrer's Los Angeles house testifies to her fondness for white. The interior designer sees white as a clean slate, like a writer approaching a blank piece of paper. But not all of her whites are created equal— where some people may see a monochrome, Scherrer sees nuanced depth. "I mix whites according to my mood and state of mind," she says. "No other color is as diversified—spiritual or sharp and crisp; soft and muted; gracefully aged; airy and breezy; bright and sparkling."

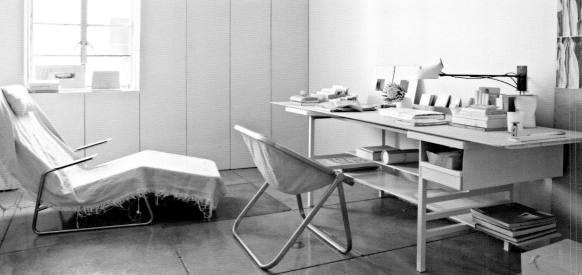

HARMONIOUS:
E PLURIBUS UNUM

I'VE NEVER
SEEN A
PIECE OF
UPHOLSTERY
THAT DIDN'T
LOOK BETTER
IN WHITE.

ANN HOLDEN

Alberto Campo Baeza's 2009 Between Cathedrals project in Cádiz, Spain, proposes suspending a white steel plaza/viewing platform between the new and old cathedrals in the city's thirteenth-century courtyard. According to the architect, the "white and simple architecture attempts to achieve everything with almost nothing."

White is democratic. It is versatile. It feels at home in any room of the house, from closet to kitchen to cathedral-ceilinged atrium. White is simultaneously honest and refined, grand and unassuming. It is both a quick fix and an enduring act of commitment.

Without any effort whatsoever, white marries architecture from different periods. "When two adjacent buildings have a white skin, their pure and abstract nature is revealed," says architect Charles Bohl. It also bridges aesthetics: in eighteenth-century Sweden, whites, grays, and pale blues provided the basis for the Gustavian style, a distilled appropriation of the ornate, gilded courts of Versailles.

Scottish architect Charles Rennie Mackintosh's white interiors had a seminal influence on design at the turn of the twentieth century, and by the late 1920s, the reductive style of the modern movement began to emerge. It designated white as the color best suited to the open plan, in which traditional rooms were replaced with free, flowing spaces.

In her own way, Elsie de Wolfe championed Mackintosh's philosophy in her 1911 decorating bible, *The House in Good Taste*. With a single, memorable phrase—"I believe in plenty of optimism and white paint"—she ushered in an era of egalitarian design that looked to the future, not to the past.

Around the same time, British decorator Syrie Maugham's decisive and prolific use of white enabled her to combine every conceivable material, period, and finish in her upscale projects. She pickled her clients' floors white; she whitened antique Louis XV chairs and obliterated the patina of even earlier pieces by bleaching them until they resembled "sun-blanched bones." Photographer Cecil Beaton recalled that "white sheepskin rugs were strewn over eggshell-surface floors; huge white sofas were flanked with white crackled-paint tables; and white peacock feathers were put into white vases against a white wall."

Decades later, in the 1980s, California designer Michael Taylor acknowledged his homage to Maugham when white became the signature color of his unpretentious interiors. As was the case with his mentor, white allowed him to break design rules. It lets outdoor furniture live inside; it gives antiques permission to sit beside kitschy thrift shop finds; it weds the traditional to the contemporary, the ornate to the earthy. To use a phrase coined by Andrée Putman, it reconciles "poor materials" with "rich."

Designer Jacques Garcia mixed period styles in one of his recent seating collections, using white upholstery to unite the group's cosmopolitan shapes. "It set off the generosity of a curve, the taut line of a leg, or the beautiful line of a curule," he says, "so that all the pieces conversed with more clarity and determination."

Steven Holl's 2007 Bloch Building, an addition to the Nelson-Atkins Museum of Art in Kansas City, Missouri, marries two radically different styles. His luminescent glass structures emerge from a curved lawn alongside the original 1933 Beaux-Arts building.

A conversion of two floors of a former Gorgonzola factory, Paola Navone's Milanese duplex is both colorful and white. Her white marble dining table sits on a paved concrete floor opposite a wall of illuminated zinc shelves that showcase a collection of terra-cotta vessels, celadon figurines, and tin candlesticks. In a gesture she sees as "non-design design," she shielded the windows from passersby with a sail-sized white scrim held in place by a handful of giant nails.

Work Architecture turned a former storefront and two subfloors in Tribeca, New York, into a kinetic loft where levels shift and rooms transition across a translucent bridge. Plum-colored concrete floors, mesquite tiles, and felt walls contrast sharply with the space's main entry, which is glossy, sun drenched, and white. The gallery wall showcases an art collection that includes photographs by William Wegman and Ruth Orkin.

The only light in the dining room of designer Tricia Foley's Long Island, New York, weekend house comes from a nineteenth-century chandelier and faux-bois sconces. A stack of Wedgwood china, some of which Foley designed, hints at a vast collection of white place settings that, she reckons, could easily outfit a dinner party for two hundred.

In the living room of a reclaimed 1860s Boston row house, architects Katarina Edlund and Scott Slarsky contrasted an ornate ceiling and moldings with the minimal sheers that cover the windows. White pulls together a seemingly disparate group of furnishings: sleek, white leather sofa, cabriole-legged armchairs, Scandinavian grandfather clock, and classical plaster foot.

Benjamin Noriega-Ortiz often uses white to fuse formally different shapes. In this Manhattan apartment, he paired a sleek bone table and simply upholstered benches with rococo Egyptian chairs.

In a Hamptons house, the walls, Jerusalem stone floors, and shag carpeting all match sand that Noriega-Ortiz gathered from a nearby beach. A lighter shade of upholstery dresses Italian sofas and blonde Chippendale chairs.

Abstract white spaces without apparent material complexities hold no appeal for architect Eric Gartner. When clients requested an all-white palette for their Manhattan penthouse, he constructed a stratum of bleached floors, Anigre cabinetry, textured limestone walls, marble kitchen counters, and acid-etched glass partitions. Charles Allem added still more dimension by accenting the white furnishings with silver. He mingled contours with right angles, marbles with silks, and swathed Arne Jacobsen Egg chairs in lambskin.

Darryl Carter's room-to-room scheme of bleached-oak floors and white walls makes this Bal Harbour, Florida, apartment feel more like a loft. Located on the twenty-fourth floor overlooking palm trees and the Atlantic Ocean, the master bedroom pairs an organic sculpture and cowhide rug with a graphic four-poster bed and vintage Z chair. "White makes a formal setting approachable," says Carter, "and it neutralizes spatial and stylistic boundaries."

Throughout a beach house on Florida's Gulf Coast, architect Bates Corkern and interior designer Liz Hand Woods used white walls and breezy linen drapes to bridge the potentially conflicting contemporary and traditional tastes of the owners. In this dining room, a cabinet upholstered in white leather floats off the wall in true modernist style, setting off a set of klismoslike French chairs.

"Absence of color," says architect Lee Ledbetter, "forces our attention to form, shadows, texture, light." Hung above a grand piano in his New Orleans living room, the otherworldly white light in Hiroshi Sugimoto's photograph *Bay of Sagami, Atami* corrals a group of white objects together, including Peter Lane's birch-bark ceramic vessel, Frank Gehry's porcelain candlesticks, and a Nymphenburg porcelain skull.

Jacques Garcia's unusual mix of inspirations includes Zen minimalism and Napoleon III extravagance. "I often think in red," says the designer, "but that doesn't prevent me from loving white." He uses white to unify his furniture and accessories collection for Baker: a Murano glass lamp base resembles bamboo; a porcelain urn has a smooth white glaze; a cabinet is leafed in silver and gold.

Like all the rooms in Jennifer Post's 1904 Manhattan apartment, the formal dining room is dressed top-to-bottom in white. "You either 'get' white or you don't," says the designer. "Like us all, I am bombarded with technology, and as soon as I open the door to my apartment, I'm hit with the enveloping calmness and sense of silence white brings."

Architects Tsao & McKown left the curvaceous cove of the stairwell in this mid-nineteenth-century townhouse unadorned so that it offset the period formality of the original balustrade and entry hall. A fifth-floor oculus sheds light onto a ribbonlike metal sculpture installed next to the stair.

Marina Toscano's streamlined Alexandria floor lamp is a contemporary beacon for traditional damask and crystal chandelier necklaces.

Jonathan Adler espouses what he calls a "happy chic" philosophy in his books; he practices what he preaches in his interior design. He considers orange to be a neutral and once said, "If I were a doctor I would prescribe yellow to cure all ills." In a twinkling and surreal white corner of this Manhattan master bedroom, a Chippendale chair cozies up to a baroque mirror and a classical bust.

With a wry sense of humor, Marcel Wanders designed this Palma de Mallorca bedroom vignette as a smoke-and-mirrors visual pun. Wanders's desk/vanity reflects Maarten Baas's charred Smoke chair against an army of sleek white surfaces.

Decorative flourishes and a rhythm of dark and light surfaces warm up the angular lines of a house on the outskirts of Minneapolis. Architects Julie Snow and Connie Lindor turned one wall of an otherwise white master bathroom into a graphic focal point by installing a pixelated mural made from Bisazza mosaic tiles.

White-lacquered wall panels, marble floor tiles, and stainless-steel shelving and fireplace surround reflect southern light throughout the living room of this apartment in San Francisco's Nob Hill. Designer Orlando Diaz-Azcuy's white shell unites the owners' eclectic collection of art and furnishings. There is no hint that Fabio Novembre's rope-legged table and a print from Damien Hirst's dot series were conceived centuries apart from a pair of Louis XV armchairs.

OVERLEAF
Miami-based designer Nacho Polo breaks any autocratic interior design rule he comes across. He rescued a floor of an early-nineteenth-century building in Madrid, compensating for a string of poor renovations by eliminating walls and installing period moldings. White fuses every style from baroque to midcentury modern, neoclassical to industrial, excessive Victorian to edgy Italian.

NEUTRAL:
FROM GENERIC TO GLAMOROUS

French designer Andrée Putman's 1984 treatment of beige in an office for the Minister of Culture in Bordeaux was at the time as shocking as Syrie Maugham's treatment of white decades earlier. In her renovation, Putman didn't conform to the room's eighteenth-century gilt paneling and shied away from Louis XV armchairs and taffeta drapes. Instead, she installed a suite of shapely, minimalist tables and chairs and hung high-waisted, billowy panels on the windows, all in an effort to "drown the room in light beige which ends up adding a sort of humor to this terribly serious space."

IF TIME WERE A COLOR, I BET IT WOULD BE A TASTEFUL OFF-WHITE.

GREG PARRISH

Syrie Maugham's London house, designed in the 1920s, is known for its iconic white drawing room; in reality, like many designers, Maugham called on a broad spectrum of whites and beiges to give the space depth and dimension. "That kind of assemblage does two opposite things," says interior designer Alexa Hampton. "The similarities soothe while the disparate shades energize. There's nothing like some well-orchestrated hypocrisy!"

Anyone who uses the words "vanilla" or "beige" to describe something as bland or boring is oblivious to the potential of white and its infinite off-white complements. While cautioning against overuse, legendary interior decorator Albert Hadley staunchly defended beige as supremely atmospheric. "It's bisque," he once said, "it's ivory; it's cream; it's stone; it's toast; it's cappuccino. It's, well, it's magic!"

The word *beige*, a catchall for everything whitish, derives from France, where it first referenced undyed cotton. Documents from 1686 record beige's darker precursor, *drab*, a four-letter word that is arguably at the root of beige's synonymy with dreariness. *Beige* and *ecru*—from the French translation of raw or unbleached—were interchangeable until the 1950s, when they garnered individual respectability and ventured out on their own.

Due to its mass appeal, beige is thought of by many as Muzak for the eyes, and it is considered to be a non-confrontational color for commonplace objects, from pantyhose to janitors' uniforms. But in the hands of an accomplished interior designer who reads beige as an earth-toned, grounded, textural counterpart to white, the color becomes chic and suave. Translated into raw silks, satins, and grass cloths, beige is elevated, taking on a glamour that has no resemblance to white's pristine and prissy characteristics.

In the late 1920s, *Vogue* editors wrote that decorator Syrie Maugham "apprehended the sweet uses of light and white" when she designed one of the most "influential rooms of the century." By today's standards her white room, which contained shades of ivory, vellum, parchment, pearl, and oyster, is decidedly buttery. "At that time, white paint still contained quantities of lead so it had a warmth to it," says design historian and Maugham biographer Pauline Metcalf.

Van Day Truex, taste arbiter, author, decorator, and Tiffany's director in the late 1950s, had a penchant for beige so strong that "Truex beige" joined the design lexicon around that time. Legendary decorator Billy Baldwin was prompted to fear that "someday Van will beige himself to death!" Tiffany's current director, John Loring, who describes himself as "very beige," lives in a beige house but adamantly qualifies its character. "There's a difference between an honest beige and a tenement beige," he says. Like Truex, he doesn't think of beige as an earth tone. "But there again," he says, "my favorite earth tone is gold!"

If Coco Chanel were still alive, she might disagree with Loring; while she valued the crispness of white in her clothing, she had a penchant for the earthiness of beige. In recent years, her company launched Beige, an elegant, nectar fragrance, based on a comment she made decades ago: "I take refuge in beige, because it's natural."

The sparsely furnished master bedroom is the most calming space in a Tribeca, New York, duplex Francine Gardner designed. Walls and cabinets are textured in a café au lait–colored plaster, and various sculptural objects reflect incoming light from the Hudson River. In sharp contrast, other rooms are seriously festive. The sitting room is a cornucopia of reds, while the spare bedroom has awning-striped floors.

Ice-white plaster walls, a beige-gray concrete floor, and mirror and etched-glass panels converge in this spare, organic bathroom Clodagh designed for a Tribeca loft. With one-inch reveals instead of baseboards, the walls appear to float—as does a sixteen-foot-long cantilevered trough sink. In contrast, a massive boulder, picked up from a local landscaper, is decidedly down-to-earth. Sliced nearly all the way through, it supports the shower's glass wall and serves as an observation perch for panoramic views of downtown Manhattan. "A neutral room," says Clodagh, "allows you to think in color."

South African designer Laurie Owen, who often collaborates with local artisans, favors natural materials when she designs interiors. The neutral palette of her Johannesburg living room includes every color from bone white to tan. In a romanticized Stone Age style, a large-scale collage of wicker, hide, and petrified woods meets felled tree trunks and pillows that resemble giant river rocks.

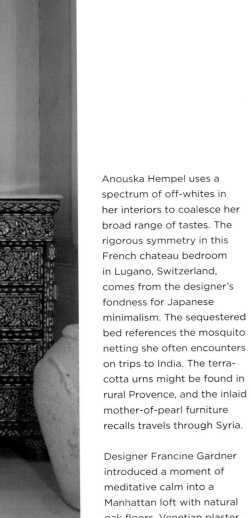

Anouska Hempel uses a spectrum of off-whites in her interiors to coalesce her broad range of tastes. The rigorous symmetry in this French chateau bedroom in Lugano, Switzerland, comes from the designer's fondness for Japanese minimalism. The sequestered bed references the mosquito netting she often encounters on trips to India. The terra-cotta urns might be found in rural Provence, and the inlaid mother-of-pearl furniture recalls travels through Syria.

Designer Francine Gardner introduced a moment of meditative calm into a Manhattan loft with natural oak floors, Venetian plaster walls, cerused cabinetry, and creamy leather upholstery. In the words of designer Lori Weitzner, "White is the color that whispers loudly."

In this Paris pied-à-terre, architect Hugh Newell Jacobsen chose an array of neutrals—natural linen to beige leather to ivory plaster—to direct visitors' attention outside onto a postcard view of the Pantheon's eighteenth-century dome. The original Marie Antoinette–style moldings were unsalvageable, giving Jacobsen carte blanche to rethink all of the surfaces; in the master bedroom he upholstered a fireplace and storage wall in oatmeal-colored linen. In the drawing room, starkly white walls provide a backdrop for a Raoul Dufy canvas and a set of framed Ming textiles.

By painting the shell of this Parisian apartment white and installing gray and beige seating, Pierre Yovanovitch underplays the precision and meticulousness of his architecture. The sculpted Thassos marble fireplace is attached to a floating wall, and a voluminous staircase spirals like a nautilus shell; both read as spontaneous flourishes. "White underlines the strength, fluidity, and sobriety of a good piece of architecture," the designer says.

Luminous white walls allow for visual harmony between sleek 1940s chairs and tribal Atlas Mountain carpets in the Chicago house John Mark designed with architect Paul Florian. "I think of white environments as liberating in the modernist sense," says Florian. "They are a neutral stage within which the pattern of our actions is heightened and thrown into relief."

By means of a mixed bag of neutrals, Andrew Flesher's prewar Minneapolis apartment is a hybrid of rustic cabin and French salon. A faux-bois table, sisal carpet, and antler chandelier encounter Venetian plaster ceilings, a fireplace surround refaced in aged mirrored glass, and a raw silk bergère.

Thomas Pheasant's furniture designs marry modern geometry and classical proportions. Here, chairs upholstered in grained ivory leather are put on display in a Baker showroom, which is kept neutral to flatter rotating collections. Pheasant also uses his light-filled house near Georgetown in Washington, D.C., to test his designs.

Designer Alexandra Angle lightened a dark, tiny Manhattan pied-à-terre by layering stark and warm whites and ecrus. A sense of depth, which invigorates the room's flat northern light, results from a hierarchy of finishes, from matte to polished.

The "hers" bathroom in a Bel Air mansion once owned by the celebrated actress Bette Davis still epitomizes vintage Hollywood glamour. Kerry Joyce customarily designs white bathrooms, but here he layered on texture and patina that is both subtle and graphic.

Style maven Marian McEvoy once described Jan Showers's aesthetic as "a generous, strategically edited mix of Hitchcockian Hollywood swank." Showers layered peach undertones into the ivory walls of this glamorous bedroom in Austin, Texas, and incorporated dressmaker details into the tailored valances and silk-tufted William Haines bed.

A fifteen-foot-long glass door opens to a fragrant high desert garden in this Trey Jordan–designed house in Santa Fe. Local craftspeople laboriously hand-troweled and -polished a subtle pearlescence into the living room's plaster gypsum walls—they might be mistaken for matte suede. "Unlike a consistently monochrome surface, this wall treatment holds rather than reflects light," says the architect, "so it adopts a golden hue at sunset and looks cooler whenever the sky is bright blue."

Parisian designer Pierre Yovanovitch crafts his fireplaces from a handful of white materials and deploys them as sculptural pieces rather than as focal points. In this Paris apartment, the angular white plaster fire surround juxtaposes with an undulating sofa as it echoes the proportions of a framed Georges Mathieu painting and a tray ceiling.

In the living room of a
Paris *hôtel particulier*,
a ceramic fire surround
Yovanovitch designed with
Armelle Benoit melts into
the floor as if it were one of
Salvador Dalí's surrealistic
clocks. A pair of 1960s
Swedish armchairs and a
1970s bronze Laverne table
sit on a circular, coffee-
colored carpet.

Set against white walls and linen drapes, the muted grays and sand tones in this spacious Long Island, New York, living room echo a foggy early morning walk to nearby beaches. Deborah Berke's austere architecture is a distillation of local historic houses and barns, and FORM Architecture's layered interiors cater to a southern light that enlivens the room throughout the day. "I love white in a 'what other color is there?' kind of way," says Berke.

A sprawling Mexican fig tree
that anchors the courtyard
of this Los Angeles house
inspired designer Barbara
Barry to create a neutral
living room. Working off the
bark's tawny undertones,
the designer installed ivory
wall paneling and a beige
French limestone fireplace.
Upholstered in oatmeal,

mushroom, and pale amber,
her furniture designs team
up with Eileen Gray's iconic
Bibendum chair. Evening
light exposes the room
to a host of tonalities. "I
love colors that can't be
described in one word
because it takes a moment
to connect to the feeling
they evoke," says Barry.

OVERLEAF
Along with a panoramic
view of the Pacific, shoreline
rocks, driftwood, and
bleached fossils dot the
backyard beach of Kelly
Wearstler's Malibu getaway.
When the designer gutted
and reconfigured the interior
of the 1990s house, those

natural elements—translated
into shades of gray, jute,
silver, and taupe—became
fodder for her surreal
and funky decor, from a
sculpture resembling a giant,
jointed crustacean to an
African plaster bust with
exploding dreadlocks.

THOUGHTFUL:
THE COLOR OF SILENCE

HEAVEN IS WHITE. THAT WHICH GETS US CLOSEST TO HEAVEN SHEDS ITS COLOR.

ANONYMOUS

The color black is missing from performance artist Yoko Ono's 1966 piece *Play It by Trust*, but otherwise it resembles a conventional chess set. Conceived as an antiwar statement, Ono's provocative use of monochrome obliterates any distinctions between players. A brass plaque on the board's underside states: "Chess set for playing as long as you can remember where all your pieces are."

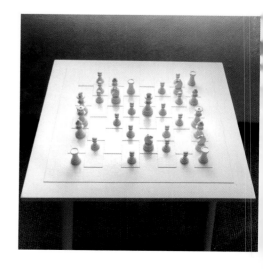

White continuously absorbs and radiates light and even appears to generate light of its own accord. Because light's presence is a metaphor for knowledge, inspiration, and enlightenment, white is strongly associated with spirituality and transcendent thought. It is the predominant color of art galleries, churches, monasteries, and museums, where its luminescence is revered. In the words of architect Richard Meier, "Light is the protagonist of our understanding and reading of space. It is the means by which we are able to experience what we call sacred."

To some, giving preference to white in places constructed specifically for contemplation or worship seems puritanical. "The negation of color in an all-white environment is a fear of decadence following Plato's thoughts of an idea being a visible form blanched of color," says architect Emanuela Frattini Magnusson. More than a century ago, in his influential *Theory of Color*, Goethe espoused similar, widely disseminated beliefs that color has special appeal for savage nations, the unrefined, and the uneducated. "Whiteness is still associated with a denial of the senses and asceticism," continues Frattini Magnusson, a critic of Goethe's morality. "It still represents the triumph of the cerebral over the sensual."

During the 1930s, New York's Museum of Modern Art rejected a centuries-old custom of displaying art against walls of saturated red, green, and blue and established an international template for showing contemporary paintings in a "white cube." To this day, a white, angular room with no paneling or moldings is considered the optimal way to decontextualize art and render it autonomous. White provides a negative space that allows color and form to take precedence.

In May 1980, artist Robert Irwin constructed a version of a white box that many onlookers refer to as a quasi-religious experience. It wasn't as provocative as *White on White*, the painting Kazimir Malevich exhibited more than sixty years earlier, but it was, arguably, as seminal. Irwin commandeered an unoccupied storefront in a derelict part of Los Angeles, adjusted its skylights, and painted its walls and ceiling an even white. He knocked out the wall facing the street and replaced it with a sheer, semi-transparent white scrim. "When I first came upon it," remembers architect Brian Murphy, "I literally dropped to my knees because it was radiating so much light." For two weeks, people communed with the piece, some for hours at a time, and when Irwin dismantled it, it was still pristine.

Art critic RoseLee Goldberg sees something intrinsically provocative in the act of using white. "It's a way for the artist to force an immediate engagement on viewers," she says. "Refusing color is an enlightening act, illusory and uplifting, having to do with luminosity and clarity." Artist Julie Levesque, who mainly works with white materials, feels it "holds a cleansing, light spirituality." She says, "It is all, and nothing at all."

Matte black is considered the signature color of Louise Nevelson's assemblages, which she created from discarded scraps of metal and wood, but she sometimes painted them gold or white. In 1977, for a permanent installation in the five-sided Chapel of the Good Shepherd in Saint Peter's Lutheran Church in Manhattan, the artist hung white friezes on white walls to symbolize the twelve apostles and the holy trinity. The chapel, with its bleached-ash furniture and frosted-glass windows, still serves as a meditative respite from the bustle of Lexington Avenue. "If you go deep into any religion," Nevelson once said, "you arrive at the same harmony."

Robert Irwin first began hanging scrims in what he terms "site-conditioned installations" in the early 1970s. In his 2007 work *Five x Five*, five white panels were suspended perpendicular to five black panels, each one separated by a walkway. When viewed up close, the edges and structure of each 250-square-foot scrim disappeared, leaving viewers to re-experience the gallery's light and space. Irwin wants his art to transcend its materiality and extend the limits of thought and perception. "Color provokes a psychic vibration," painter and art theorist Wassily Kandinsky once said. "Color hides a power still unknown but real, which acts on every part of the human body."

Robert Ryman's work utilizes every conceivable viscosity, finish, and texture of white. "White has a tendency to make things visible," he has said. In a lit white gallery, his canvases appear to hover in place rather than hang: "If you were to see any of my paintings off of the wall, they would not make any sense at all." Artist and writer David Batchelor sees vibrancy in Ryman's work. "His whites are colors," he wrote. "His whites are empirical whites. Above all, his whites are plural." One critic once referred to Ryman's monochrome as "painting's endgame," but to the artist white is the color of self-exploration.

Architect John Pawson originally contemplated carving the central room in "Plain Space," his 2011 retrospective exhibition at London's Design Museum, from a massive hunk of white chalk, but instead he opted for light, sheetrock, and muslin screens. Benches flank two white walls that rise to a softly lit barrel ceiling, while a glowing white halo surrounds the doorway. "There are fifty different color shades of white," Pawson once said, "and you could probably only see them in an empty room."

Pawson's sculptural use of white provokes a sense of spatial clarity, silence, and asceticism. In Our Lady of Nový Dvùr, a 2004 conversion of a derelict estate west of Prague into a monastery for a closed order of Cistercian monks, light filters through sculptural openings and seems to dissolve the solidity of the lime-washed plaster surfaces. Vaulted ceilings merge into a shapeless, limitless white that is both mysterious and exhilarating.

"Boiseries," a bleached, full-scale interpretation of a suite from Paris's Hôtel de Crillon installed at New York's Metropolitan Museum of Art, is an abstraction of one of the museum's eighteenth-century rooms. Icelandic sculptor Katrin Sigurdardottir's pale-by-comparison rendition, with its ghostly hand-carved paneling and period furniture, prompted *New York Times* art reviewer Ken Johnson to ponder whether "the uncontaminated whiteness" reflected the era of the French Enlightenment.

British ceramic artist Edmund de Waal perceives the subtle modulations within his register of white glazes, from celadon to gray, as a "touchstone of tonality," or the visual opposite of noise. Unlike most ceramicists, de Waal's work rarely ends up on plinths. In his 2002 *Porcelain Rooms*, an installation at the Geffrye Museum in London, one wall of stacked shelves held 360 small pots, some indented or pinched and all glazed in an ethereal range of celadons. In *A Sounding Line*, a 2010 display at Chatsworth, a baroque country house in Derbyshire, de Waal positioned sixty-six white and cream glazed jars on mantels and corbels and along corridors. De Waal still has the first plain cylinder he made when he was five years old. "It's very, very, very heavy," he has said, "and very, very, very white."

Cleansing is a prominent ritual in many religions. During the Festival of Lights, or Diwali, an annual Hindu festival native to several countries throughout Asia, a standard purification ritual for Jain worshippers is to clean statues. Here, in the south of India, a sixty-foot-tall deity, carved from a solid block of granite, is streaked with the aftermath of a milk and yogurt bath.

In Bhutan, Buddhists house sacred relics in dome-shaped chortens or stupas, which are considered to be architectural representations of the path to enlightenment. According to *The Legend of the Great Stupa Jarungkhasor*, "Whoever gives a coat of whitewash to the Stupa acquires a fair and lustrous complexion, happiness, prosperity and health, attaining predominance over men, gods and demons."

Whether he uses bleached animal bones, stones, or twigs in his sculptures, British artist Andy Goldsworthy demonstrates nature's beauty and impermanence. His customary "studio" may be a snow bank, quarry, forest, desert, or riverbed; at times, he also works indoors. In his 2007 *White Walls*, Goldsworthy plastered the interior walls of Galerie Lelong, in New York, with moist white porcelain from Cornwall, United Kingdom, where he was born. Over the course of five weeks, the substance dried, cracked, flaked, and crumbled, and the formerly static walls echoed the transience of nature.

Certain artists use white to connote otherworldliness. As a young boy, Finnish sculptor Kim Simonsson molded his first backyard statue out of snow. Inspired by Japanese manga comics, he now carves large glass-eyed figures of children out of white clay. Covered with white auto paint, the sculptures take on a strangely enchanted, spectral appearance.

Millions of sheets of blank white paper, falling like dried leaves and crunching underfoot like newly fallen snow, resembled a choreographed dream sequence in *Corpus*, the light and sound installation artist Ann Hamilton created in 2004 for the Massachusetts Museum of Contemporary Art. Pneumatic mechanisms secured in the rafters high overhead released the paper—one sheet at a time—into the football-field-sized gallery. During the ten-month-long piece, horn-shaped speakers descended to amplify a soundtrack of twenty-four voices as magenta-silk-covered windows cast a pink light throughout the room.

White can be clinical, antiseptic, and beautifully ice cold, as in the tongue-in-cheek dining room designer Amy Lau created for a Showtime show house as a fantasy domicile for the protagonist of the channel's award-winning series *Dexter*. Lau corralled a team of artisans and artists, including Gregoire Abrial, Stephen Antonson, Thomas Fuchs, and Steve Butcher, and orchestrated a space that manifested the inner workings of Dexter Morgan, the show's charming, psychopathic, serial-killer star. Here, white translates an obsession with cleanliness and a neurotic meticulousness. Angelica Bergamini's window installation, a delicate crochet of monofilament fishing line and glass beads, exemplified the fragility of life.

The sharp contrast between white and shade accentuates and articulates curved shapes. Mounted in direct southern light on interior designer Juan Montoya's massive, tapering plinth, Eva Hild's paper-thin ceramic sculpture is all contours and light.

Illuminated by a bank of frosted-glass windows and an overhead skylight, architect Ron Goldman's spiral staircase appears to float as it undulates up three flights of a Malibu house. Seventeen of Bertjan Pot's hanging light fixtures, placed randomly by designer Jamie Bush, cast spidery evening shadows.

Richard Meier's belief that white conveys optimism and hope is evidenced in his 2003 Jubilee Church. Located on a flat, fan-shaped site in Tor Tre Teste, a suburb of Rome, the building seems to vibrate with white light at certain times of the day. Its geometry deflects direct sun and dapples the interior with a transcendent, calming illumination. Sail-like concrete exterior walls soar as high as ninety feet and contain a titanium dioxide pigment that accelerates natural oxidation so that the self-cleaning marblelike surface is perpetually luminous. Inside, a nineteenth-century cross mounted above the main altar punctuates a controlled palette of materials—travertine, glass, pale timber, and stucco—amplifying the already exalted air of reverence and serenity.

Whiteness, light, and principles of proportion are the chief characteristics of Hanrahan Meyers's 2010 design of the four-thousand-square-foot sanctuary at the Infinity Chapel at the Tenth Church of Christ, Scientist in Manhattan. The architects used sacred geometries of squares and golden-section triangles to carve spherically curved walls that seem to trap infinite amounts of self-perpetuating light.

OVERLEAF
White enables artist Julie Levesque to freeze memories and impose an emotional narrative onto everyday objects. In a 2002 installation, *What Remains*, she transformed the Provincetown Art Association and Museum into a memory of her second-grade classroom. White fluorescent light projected from a ruined white "blackboard" highlighted twenty stark white desks—nine were intact and the rest were bowed—and coats of salt "preserved" books, pencils, and poster-sized yearbook pictures.

NATURAL:
BETWEEN
HEAVEN
AND
EARTH

Photographer Vincent Munier's image of two polar bears speaks to one of the animal's unique features: the fur appears white, but the coarse hairs of the topcoat as well as the thinner hairs of the undercoat are actually hollow and semi-transparent. The fur, or rather the spaces within each hair, reflects all of the visible wavelengths of sunlight, so that the human eye sees white.

White is at the core of existence. Bones and skeletons, the supporting structures of all things living and breathing, are a shade of white. Mothers' milk is white, as are many eggshells, regardless of the color of the bird that lays them or hatches from them.

While Moby-Dick, Herman Melville's great albino whale, ranks as literature's most sinister evocation of the color, other white animals—real or mythical—are beloved, revered, and prized for their rarity. Often considered sacred or magical, they inspire legends and superstitions. The valiant white steed, sometimes in the guise of a unicorn or a winged Pegasus, exemplifies wisdom and moral rectitude. White elephants are doted upon as symbols of prosperity and longevity.

In Native American lore, a wise white owl's feather is a coveted token of bravery. In Scotland, white deer embody the noblest characteristics of royalty and are sought but almost never hunted. To the traditional Chinese, white doves are both delegates of peace and a choice ingredient in an immune-boosting soup.

Aside from dove soup tonic and life-nurturing milk, white food is not generally perceived as nutritious, and those who partake of it, according to style maven Diana Vreeland, are not particularly ambitious or inspired. "People who eat white bread," she liked to say, "have no dreams!" Processed foods aside, naturally white edibles— with the exceptions of horseradish and garlic, among a few others—tend not to have distinctive tastes.

If nature withholds flavor from white food, it favors flowering white plants by endowing them with intoxicating scents. In general, blossoms rely on their color to seduce pollinators; nature gave the gift of perfume to white freesia, jasmine, and tuberose as if in compensation for a lack of pigment. Certain white blooms wait for dark, when moths abound, before their petals open and release their fragrance, which is why moon gardens are so seductive at night.

Snow glows day and night not from its inherent whiteness but from the light-diffusing composition of frozen, transparent water crystals. This is one reason painters throughout history, from Peter Paul Rubens to Jean-Paul Riopelle, have insisted that true, pure white does not exist in nature—a belief no doubt supported by Frank Lloyd Wright. In a 1958 letter to a *New York Times* art critic, he railed against a campaign to paint the Guggenheim Museum's galleries "dead-white"; he felt this would tear "the inside from the outer walls of the organic building." Many architects subscribe to Wright's philosophy that "Buildings, too, are children of Earth and Sun."

THE SNOW DOESN'T GIVE A SOFT WHITE DAMN WHOM IT TOUCHES.
E. E. CUMMINGS

Since the 1950s Jack Lenor Larsen has designed crisp cottons, heavy linens, and pearly silks inspired by seemingly unremarkable items—a deserted beach, or a torn-paper collage. Shapes and textures derived from nature crop up throughout the extensive collection of textiles and crafts in his Park Avenue, New York, apartment. "The sparkling white of trumpet lilies is perhaps my favorite 'bright,'" he once said.

A flat, snowy surface is perceived as uniformly white because the light hitting it reflects back without favoring any one color. Snow was the prerequisite for several artists and architects who built structures for "Snow Show," an exhibition held in Lapland, Finland, in 2004, in temperatures of negative forty-five degrees Celsius, and photographed by Davis. British artist Rachel Whiteread, who characteristically casts containers out of resin, plaster, and concrete, collaborated with Finnish architect Juhani Pallasmaa to produce a small, quiet fortress from blocks of compacted snow. Inside, a complex stepped landscape defied the exterior's simplicity.

White marble is just one of the many natural phenomena that have drawn the attention of photographer Lynn Davis. The excavation of the mines in Carrara began more than two thousand years ago. Statuary marble, Carrara's purest yield, is 98 percent calcium carbonate, has virtually no veins, and features a low refraction index that permits light to penetrate the stone, resulting in a waxy look that mimics human flesh. The whiter the marble, the greater its value.

Antoine Bootz's meditative
photograph of fog and
low-lying mist is explained
only in part by suspended
drops of water and ice
crystals. The daytime sky
appears blue because the
atmosphere scatters
the light from the sun; as
it travels and approaches
infinity, it looks whiter and
whiter. "It is not the clear-
sighted who rule the world,"
wrote Joseph Conrad.
"Great achievements are
accomplished in a blessed,
warm fog."

Stephen Antonson continues an ancient craft tradition when he fashions chalky white gypsum into frames, screens, and tables with antelope legs. Here, the designer brushed liquid plaster onto the wire armature of his Icicle Chandelier until it started to drip and resemble a severe case of frostbite.

White-glazed porcelain deftly showcases the textures and throwing lines of Kathy Erteman's work, shown here on a Lori Weitzner textile. Erteman sliced off the vessel's base when it was fresh from the wheel, nudged the resulting cylinder into an organic warp, and set it on a new base. Once dried, the ceramicist refined its contours and, weeks later, applied three white glazes—satin matte inside, textured white outside, and a liquid slip that leaves traces of random circles. "Clay comes from the earth, so I feel I'm essentially modifying nature," says Erteman.

Truly white horses—those with white skin—are rare, but all white horses are held in high esteem. Many cultures and mythologies depict spectral white horses as virtuous, noble, heroic, virile, moral, or pure. They drive chariots into the sun. They emerge from churning seas or bolts of lightning. They breathe fire or restore fertility to a barren land. They are immortal or, at the very least, prophetic. Bob Tabor's photographs show that these legendary beasts are not so distant from the animals he depicts.

In general, perfectly white clouds hover in higher altitudes where subzero temperatures freeze their water content into ice crystals. Wispy, transparent cirrus clouds form above twenty thousand feet; lumpy clouds that fly too low to freeze release the water molecules as drizzle and rain.

Ceremonial Cameroon juju hats, a splay of feathers sewn into a circular raffia base, generally reference the nobility of birds, but to a host of other cultures white feathers symbolize pacifism, cowardice, or bravery. A single, floating feather is sometimes viewed as a message from a dearly departed; in combination, they are the stuff of angels' wings. In a chronology of color, dated 1821, grayish white is defined as "inside quill feathers of the kittiwake," snow white as "breast of the black headed gull," and orange white as "breast of white or screech owl."

Parisian artist Christian
Astuguevieille's designs range
from jewelry to fragrances to
candelabra. The spines and
undulating contours of his
Aton commode and Milukan
armchair are configured
by securing his signature
white-painted cord onto
wood forms. The ethereal
but practical pieces have a
tribal primitivism and call
to mind sea foam—and its
impermanence.

Rows of billowing white panels articulated a temporary art installation designed by artist and landscape architect Martha Schwartz for the 1997 Spoleto Festival. Installed on the property of an 1850s white-pillared house on McLeod Plantation in Charleston, South Carolina, *Field Work* focused on a small row of former slave cabins. At right angles to an allée of oak trees, Schwartz pegged sheet after sheet onto a network of washing lines that extended into a field of sweet grass. The fact that white, according to African spirituality, signifies the afterlife prompted one onlooker to imagine a "huge processional of ghosts."

Andy Goldsworthy's environmental art showcases the transitions of nature; in order to build with snow or ice, he needs temperatures below the freezing point. He formed the tapering spikes of this ephemeral artwork in stages, holding small amounts of snow and water in place until all the elements solidified. Built on an isolated rock surrounded by seawater, the completed sculpture resembled a starburst and lasted for as long as the sun kept its distance.

Sequence of entry is all-important in Hugh Newell Jacobsen's pavilion-style residences. In 1997 he referenced farmhouses and barns in his Nef House, an enclave of small buildings in the bucolic rolling hills of the Berkshires in Massachusetts; existing views determined the exact site and angle of each interconnecting structure. The entry walkway passes through a geometrically planted grove of pear trees, and Jacobsen honored a Quaker tradition by painting the inner side of an entry door red. Otherwise, all walls are snowy white.

Guests who venture inside Alberto Campo Baeza's 2005 Guerrero House through the rectangular building's only opening find themselves in an open-air courtyard that leads into a glass living room and a duplicate courtyard beyond. Viewed from inside and out, the house, which occupies a six-thousand-square-foot plot on the outskirts of Cádiz, Spain, is wholly white. Its solid, twenty-six-foot-high exterior walls are intriguingly windowless and lead passersby to question whether the structure might be a nunnery rather than a weekend house. To its architect, it is a clear, well-balanced manifestation of a "luminous shadow."

Located on a private island off Miami Beach, Chad Oppenheim's minimalist white residence, Villa Allegra, nestles into a tropical grove of indigenous palms, fragrant jasmine, and oleander. Its monumental keystone facade reflects into a zero-edge pool, as do visiting iguanas, egrets, and parrots, while its voluminous interior features wide doorways, expansive white walls, and the barest essentials of furniture. "I use white so much in my work," says the architect, "because it vividly celebrates the contrast between the man-made and the natural."

A white bench designed by Glass Kramer Löbbert Architects in 2008 was initially conceived as a temporary albeit practical sculpture at the German Aerospace Center, outside Cologne, but is now a permanent fixture. The firm, which consulted with Uta Graff Architects and Levin Monsigny Landscape Architects, devised a steel-frame support for a plywood substructure and Corian veneer. Spanning as wide as sixty-five feet, it is sited at the heart of the campus where it encloses a copse of copper beech, maple, and hornbeam trees. "White supplies a tension and interplay between a clearly manufactured rectangle and its green surroundings," says Löbbert.

Many painters, including Georgia O'Keeffe, see the sun-bleached bones of cows and other animals as mystical, enduring relics. "To me," the artist once said, "they are as beautiful as anything I know." Designer Vicente Wolf agrees, which is why he prizes this group of animal skulls, souvenirs of his travels in Thailand, India, Tasmania, and Namibia.

Sebastian Knorr of tecArchitecture thinks of the dramatic, eleven-foot-wide staircase he designed for a Mediterranean villa as a "naked structure." Its white engineered-wood carcass and glass railings join a terrace to the house's back garden and might well be mistaken for the excavated spine of a giant dinosaur.

Ellen Silverman's still lifes of flowers illuminate the hidden meanings the Victorians assigned to the blooms. Peonies symbolized shame and bashfulness; white lilacs, youthful innocence; white poppies, consolation; white lilies, purity; white roses, eternal love; white carnations, faithfulness; white violets, modesty; white gardenias, secret romance; white magnolias, dignity.

By the early nineteenth century, archaeological excavations proved that statuary from ancient Rome and Greece was originally painted in many colors, not left the natural white of the marble. Artist Stephen Antonson built a cream pie out of white plaster; as it was about to set, he squashed it into the face of an appropriated bust of Pan, the Greek god of nature. Far from a statement about statuary or environmental ruination, *Pie'd Pan* is simply a visual pun and a commentary on white.

OVERLEAF
A small army of glass vitrines in Ted Muehling's Manhattan workshop hold the beautiful flotsam and jetsam that inform the shapes of his jewelry, porcelain, and glassware. "Rocks, shells, eggs, and insects all inspire me and humble me," Muehling has said. Unlike other colors, white never distracts the designer from uncovering "the invisible forms that exist between nature and our perceptions of it." The Volute bowl he created for Porzellan Manufaktur Nymphenburg, for instance, is crafted from fine white porcelain.

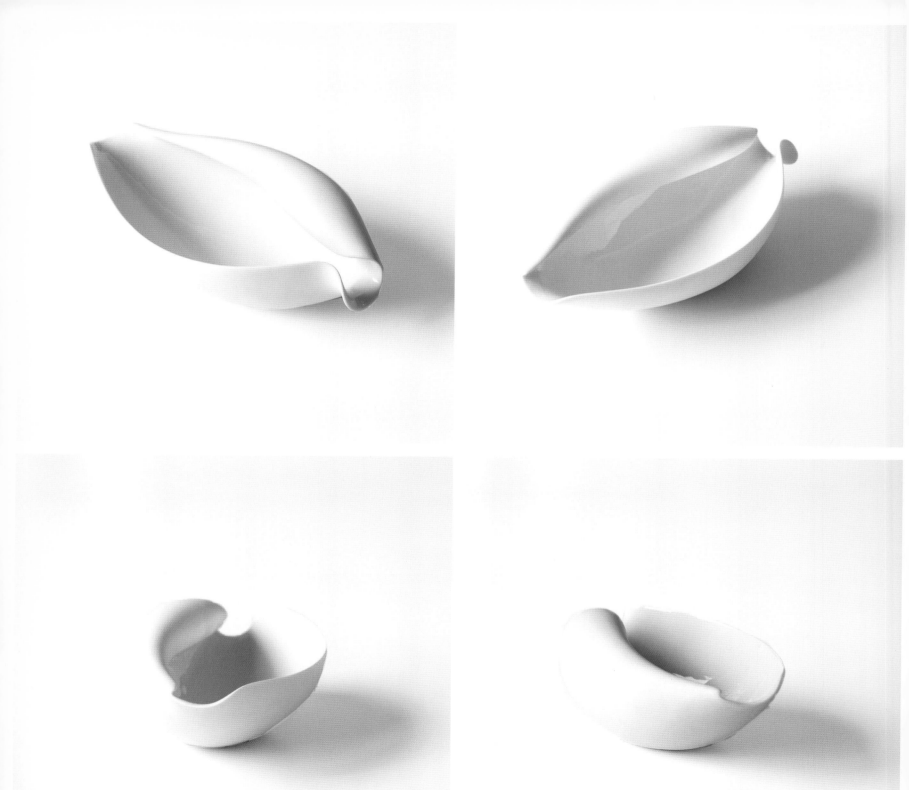

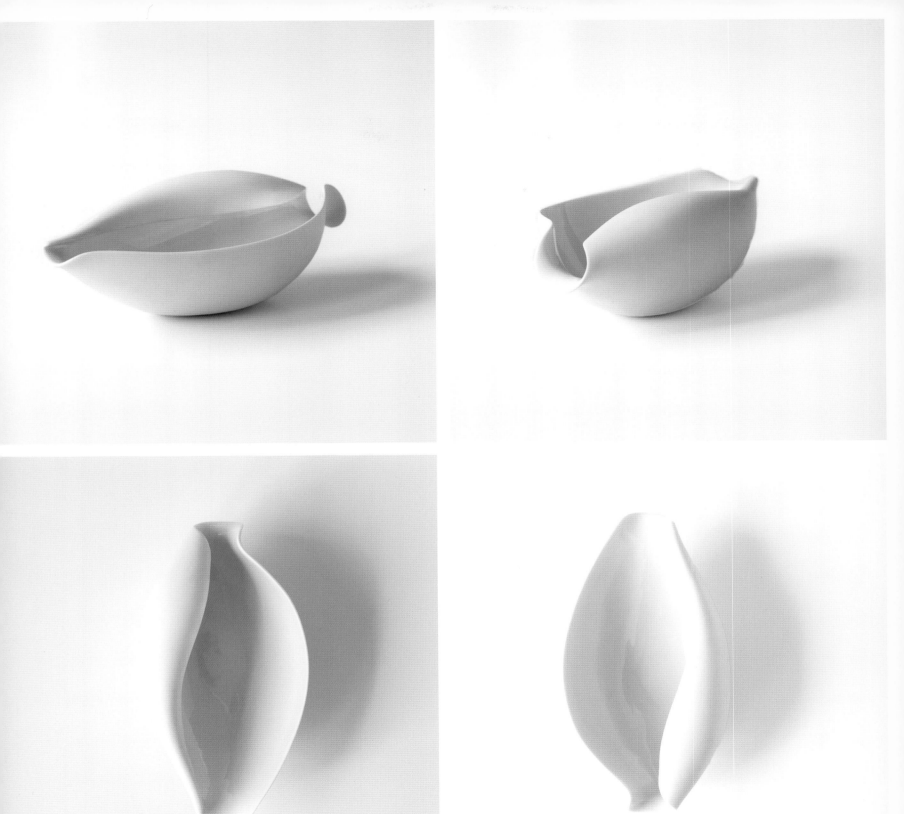

PHOTOGRAPHY CREDITS
Numbers refer to page numbers.

David S. Allee: 123

Courtesy B&B Italia: 19 left

Quentin Bacon, reprinted with permission from *Metropolitan Home* magazine, copyright Hachette Filipacchi Media U.S.: 114, 128

Alexandre Bailhache, reprinted with permission from *Metropolitan Home* magazine, copyright Hachette Filipacchi Media U.S.: 154, 155

Courtesy Baker Furniture: 135, 160

Roland Bernath, courtesy Smolenicky & Partner Architecture: 73

Hélène Binet, courtesy Edmund de Waal Studio: 180, 181

Emmanuelle Blanc: 2 top right, 66, 67

Antoine Bootz: 30, 46, 47 left, 58, 72, 96, 97, 106 right, 133, 136–37, 200–201, 206

Antoine Bootz, reprinted with permission from *Metropolitan Home* magazine, copyright Hachette Filipacchi Media U.S.: 124, 148, 149, 153, 168

Courtesy Sergio Bruns: 64, 65

Jorge Bustos, courtesy Grupo Habita: 74

Santi Caleca for DuPont Corian: 23

Javier Callejas: 75

Javier Callejas, courtesy Campo Baeza Studio: 122

Photo by Chia Chong and Adam Kuehl, from *Perfect Porches: Designing Welcoming Spaces For Outdoor Living*, by Paula S. Wallace, used by permission of Clarkson Potter/Publishers, an imprint of the Crown Publishing Group, a division of Random House, Inc.: 214

Grey Crawford: 106 left

Grey Crawford, reprinted with permission from *Metropolitan Home* magazine, copyright Hachette Filipacchi Media U.S.: 115, 164–65

Billy Cunningham, courtesy Juan Montoya Design: 188

Courtesy Cyrus Company: 70

Ian Dobbie: 68

Carlos Domenech, reprinted with permission from *Metropolitan Home* magazine, copyright Hachette Filipacchi Media U.S.: 43 right, 62 right

Colleen Duffley, reprinted with permission from *Metropolitan Home* magazine, copyright Hachette Filipacchi Media U.S: 118

John Ellis: 103

Aaron Fedor, courtesy Tori Golub Interior Design: 31, 43 left, 110

Elizabeth Felicella: 26, 125

Jen Fong: 20, 138

Marili Forastieri: 55, 126

John Reed Forsman, reprinted with permission from *Metropolitan Home* magazine, copyright Hachette Filipacchi Media U.S.: 142

Koji Fujii/Nacasa & Partners, Inc.: 90

Courtesy Jean-Marc Gady: 13

Courtesy Gallery Vetri D'Arte: 139

David Garcia, reprinted with permission from *Metropolitan Home* magazine, copyright Hachette Filipacchi Media U.S.: 44

Francine Gardner: 183

Susan Gilmore, reprinted with permission from *Metropolitan Home* magazine, copyright Hachette Filipacchi Media U.S.: 159

Jefunne Gimpel, courtesy Kim Simonsson: 186 left

Courtesy Glass Kramer Löbbert Architects: 215

Andy Goldsworthy: 210

Copyright Andy Goldsworthy, courtesy Galerie Lelong, New York: 184, 185

John Granen: 107 left

John Granen, reprinted with permission from *Metropolitan Home* magazine, copyright Hachette Filipacchi Media U.S.: 52 left, 100–101

Peter Grant: 76

Art Gray: 41

François Halard, courtesy Kelly Wearstler Design: 2 bottom left, 102, 170, 171

Roland Halbe, courtesy Campo Baeza Studio: 212–13

Ken Hayden, courtesy Rene Gonzalez Architects: 19 right

Amr Helmy, courtesy DuPont Corian: 22

Courtesy Anouska Hempel Design: 80, 81, 152

Edward Hendricks, courtesy Ministry of Design: 78, 79

Adam Heneghan, courtesy Kara Mann Design: 60–61

Laura Hull: 2 middle center, 12, 120, 121

Werner Huthmacher: 36, 37

Copyright 2011 Robert Irwin/Artists Rights Society (ARS), New York: 174

Jean-François Jaussaud/Lux Productions: 45, 156–57, 166, 167

Thibault Jeanson, courtesy Ann Hamilton Studio: 186 right

Courtesy Kallista: 42

Stephen Karlisch Photography: 163

Thanks many times over to Vicente Wolf for initiating my relationship with
The Monacelli Press, for guiding me through the process of creating *Brilliant*, and
for contributing his accomplished interior design and photography.

I am enormously grateful to Antoine Bootz who, in many ways, partnered me
throughout the production of *Brilliant* with his generosity, support, friendship, and
beautiful photography.

A special thanks to Laura Hull for her art, her photographic eye, and her steadfast
friendship and to Ellen Silverman for the creativity and grace she brings to each one
of her photographs.

Appreciation and gratitude to Gianfranco Monacelli for his talents and unwavering
faith in me.

I am thankful to Andrea Monfried for her support and consistency as well as
her broad range of talents and rapier wit, to Rebecca McNamara for her smarts and
skilled attention to detail, and to Claudia Brandenburg for her inspired layouts.

I'm enormously grateful to the designers, architects, artists, photographers, and
design minds who contributed their work, voice, or opinion to *Brilliant*,
especially Stephen Antonson, Yosi Barzilai, Alberto Campo Baeza, Greg Cerio,
Jonn Coolidge, Cathryne Czubek, Lynn Davis, Topher Delaney, Keith D'Mello,
John Ellis, Kathy Erteman, Jeff Felmus, Andy Goldsworthy, Art Gray, Yosh Han,
Doty Horn, Jean-François Jaussaud, Annie Kelly, Daniel Kessler, Jack Lenor Larsen,
Lee Ledbetter, Carey Lennox, Doug Levine, Michelle Litvin, Peter Margonelli,
Gilbert McCarragher, Eileen McComb, Bärbel Miebach, Carl Minchew, Michael Moran,
Moris Moreno, Ted Muehling, Vincent Munier, Lynn Schroeder, Sal Siggia,
Tim Street-Porter, Bob Tabor, Kris Tamburello, Catherine Tighe, Betty Wasserman,
Donald Wechsler, Hutton Wilkinson, and Ricky Zehavi.